THE PEACEFUL ARTS

THE PEACEFUL ARTS

Meditation • Yoga • Tai Chi • Stretching

MARK EVANS, JOHN HUDSON, PAUL TUCKER

HERMES
HOUSE

First published in 1999 by Hermes House

© Anness Publishing Limited 1999

Hermes House is an imprint of Anness Publishing Limited
Hermes House, 88-89 Blackfriars Road, London, SE1 8HA

This edition published in the USA by Hermes House, Anness Publishing Inc.,
27 West 20th Street, New York, NY 10011; (800) 354-9657

ISBN 1 84038 230 9

A CIP catalogue record for this book is available from the British Library

Publisher: Joanna Lorenz
Project Editor: Fiona Eaton
Editor: Emma Gray
Jacket Designer: Simon Wilder
Designers: Bobbie Colgate Stone, Allan Mole and Lilian Lindblom
Illustrator: Giovanna Pierce
Photographer: Don Last
Production Controller: Don Campaniello
Editorial Reader: Kate Henderson

Photography credits: Tony Stone Images: p131 (Bob Thomasen), p132 (Zigy Kaluzny), Zefa p130.

Printed and bound in Singapore

1 3 5 7 9 10 8 6 4 2

Previously published as three separate volumes: *Instant Meditation, Tai Chi* and *Instant Stretches*

CONTENTS

Using the Meditative State

MIND AND BODY: THE BALANCE OF TAI CHI

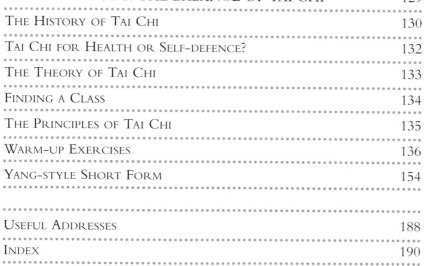

INTRODUCTION

In Eastern philosophy, the preservation of good health is placed in the context of a holistic approach to life, and in particular the concept of an energy-based system. From the idea of a universal energy, or the highest level of spirituality, down to the lowest forms of life, much of this Eastern ideology is an energetic one, with all parts of the human body interconnected and infused with a vital energy, and all life-forms similarly interdependent on an exchange of energies.

Such concepts have led to the development of traditional thera-peutic disciplines, such as Tai Chi in China and Yoga in India, which are followed as part of everyday life in order to promote self-development and to prevent illness. Both Tai Chi and Yoga connect mind and body, helping to relax muscles and release tension, while increasing your understanding of your own energies. They are skills through which you can find a way to sustain awareness and clarity in spite of the vagaries of everyday life, growing in your understanding of yourself and other people.

Many people find that their lives are so full of the demands of work, family, friends and organized leisure pursuits that they have no time to "enjoy the moment". They are so caught up in planning and working towards the future that they take little pleasure from the here and now. In their unremitting bustle they miss out on the simple pleasures of life: the change of the seasons, the singing of a bird, or the innocent wonder of a child. However beauty and joy are always there to be seen and experienced if you take the time to just watch and let the world "happen" around you.

THE INNER JOURNEY OF MEDITATION

Meditation has been in use from the beginning of time: people have always sought inner quiet and physical relaxation, for spiritual, self-realization or health reasons. It is nothing unusual, in fact it is completely natural and you do not have to be a physical contortionist to be able to achieve and enjoy the benefits of meditation at both physical and mental levels.

Rather than pushing yourself to take up some strained physical position, just relax: sit in a chair or stroll in a favourite landscape at a steady pace. It is not a good idea to slump or lie down, as this only tends to lead into sleep. It is a relaxed attentiveness that is desired. If you sit down, do so with your feet flat on the floor, hands resting in your lap or on the arms of the chair, and your head comfortably balanced. If you are walking, do so slowly and carefully, aware of the movement of each foot, and the contact with the ground beneath. Follow the example of a Buddhist monk in Sri Lanka walking up and down the same path in the forest: he moves slowly, giving total attention to his feet, the movement of his feet, changing pressures on the soles of his feet, and the reaction of the ground to his feet. This is an extremely simple but effective exercise in being truly aware of the present.

The path of meditation offers a way of becoming more awake and alive to every aspect, inner and outer, of life. The mind ceases to be a burden and distraction, and instead becomes a tool for paying very good attention to the present moment. The practice known as "mindfulness" is simply carrying this present-centred attention into your daily life and all your activities, whether you are walking, working or doing household chores. In this way, the practice of meditation can become relevant to the rest of your life, rather than being considered as something separate and isolating.

You may find meditating in a class or group helpful. In a group, you have the support of a roomful of people doing the same thing at the same time. A kind of synergy seems to exist in a group of people meditating together. However, sometimes the reverse is true and solitude is what you need to get in touch with that single-pointed attention. Time, place and companions are all matters that you can choose and experiment with.

YOGA AS PHYSICAL THERAPY

Most people tend to hold in patterns of tension arising from everyday cares and worries, bad posture or lack of exercise. These patterns make you feel stiff and unbending, and directly interfere with your movements. Inflexibility within your body can in turn affect mental flexibility, and you can become stuck in thought as well as in action. Regular stretches not only free the body, allowing you to move easily, but can also help you to think and act in a less restricted way.

By stretching your muscles, tendons and ligaments, you can make them stronger. The lengthening actions will help you to stand and walk taller and more gracefully. The joints are better supported and able to go through their full range of movements, while the muscles are better nourished from the increased blood supply. Chronic tension and contraction of the body impairs blood flow, and stretching improves this, giving added vigour and vitality.

Stretching is not a new idea: for centuries it has formed an essential part of the physical exercises that are one aspect of yoga. These exercises, including breathing techniques and meditation, have also become highly popular in the West in recent decades. There are yoga classes almost everywhere, and the best way to learn about these practices is from a trained, supportive teacher. The exercises shown are not meant in any way to be a substitute for such classes, but to give practical, simple suggestions for stretching.

One of the particular benefits of yoga stretches derives from the slow-motion movements, together with the holding of the postures, or "asana". These do not tax the heart, but help to relieve tension and strain, and conserve energy. Never overdo a movement, or strain to stretch – you should enjoy it. Practised regularly, the stretches shown in this book will improve not just your flexibility, but the overall functioning of your whole system.

You will find that the stretches demand a certain quality of mental concentration, to help steady the body and focus the mind. To help you engage your mind, concentrate on the rhythm of the movement plus the harmony of your breathing. Other techniques can also be adopted, such as working with your eyes closed or counting the length of your breath. As you become more proficient, try these methods to increase the benefit of the exercises.

THE GENTLE ART OF TAI CHI

Tai Chi Ch'uan is an ancient form of slow, graceful and rhythmic exercise which is still extremely popular in China, often being performed in public parks in the fresh morning air. It has its roots in Taoist philosophy. The movements of the Tai Chi form gently tone and strengthen the organs and muscles, improve circulation and posture, and relax both mind and body.

Its name translates as "supreme ultimate fist", but this is not its true meaning. "Strength within softness", "poetry in motion" and "moving harmony" all come closer to expressing the spirit of Tai Chi. Unlike the "hard" martial arts which rely on force and speed, Tai Chi is "soft" or "internal". Its emphasis lies in the yielding aspect of nature overcoming the hard – like the waterfall which eventually wears away the rock beneath. It teaches patience and relaxation, and fosters an understanding of the co-ordination of mind, body and spirit. It is the perfect antidote to the stresses and strains of modern life.

People of all ages, conditions and abilities can benefit from Tai Chi. No special equipment or clothing is needed, and once learned it is with you for the rest of your days - just a little regular practice is all that is needed. The entire Short Form takes only about 12 minutes to complete.

Remember how your body felt when you were a small child: loose, supple, free, full of vitality. As you get older, life's difficulties and traumas – and your responses to them - can add tension upon tension, resulting in stiffness, stress, sickness and fatigue. Practising Tai Chi regularly helps to relax your joints and muscles, releases tension, gives you a sense of spatial awareness and movement within your environment, and increases your understanding of your own and other people's energies.

INNER HARMONY: *The Art of Meditation*

MEDITATION IS ABOUT STAYING WITH THE MOMENT, being in touch with your surroundings and your inner world, much of which is more easily accessible when in the meditative state. It can be a good way of just taking time out, and allowing yourself to tune into and appreciate the moment: whether you are walking along the seashore, or sitting by a stream, or just noticing the intensity of silence in a still room and enjoying it.

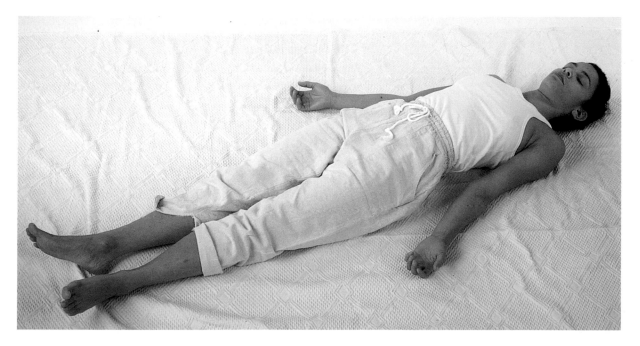

HISTORY OF MEDITATION

Meditation is perhaps most closely linked with Buddhism, and indeed it was the main practice through which its founder, Gautama, finally gained enlightenment. Buddhism has defined many stages of meditation that are practised in order to achieve the ultimate level of purifying the mind and clearing away of all thoughts and mental images.

However, one of the best-known practices of meditation is yoga, the yoking or harnessing of mental and physical powers, which is very much in the Hindu tradition. Most of us think in terms of "hatha" or royal yoga, which is a series of physical exercises and postures performed to gain physical, and therefore mental, control. Less well-known is "bhakti" yoga, which is focusing of the mind, and is akin to the style of meditation outlined here and indeed practised in the Christian faith. According to this discipline, the

practitioner sits and focuses his or her attention upon an aspect of their god. In so doing, they gain insights into their own responses to the knowledge they have of that god's powers and the lessons to be drawn from stories told of him or her.

It has long been a tradition in Christian religious communities, such as convents and monasteries, for monks or nuns to spend a period of time each day in quiet contemplation, often focusing upon a crucifix and contemplating the passion of Christ and all that it means for the believer. This is, of course, meditation, and has all the benefits of helping the individual come to an understanding of his inner beliefs and response to his faith. The practice has also become increasingly popular among lay Christians in recent years.

Right: Meditation is a part of all the world's religions. Left and below: Representations of the Buddha, which worshippers use as a focus for meditation.

THE MENTAL AND PHYSICAL BENEFITS OF MEDITATION

An individual emerging from a period of meditation, however brief, will notice a change in their emotional state from when they started their meditation exercise. This can present itself in many ways, often as a feeling of being refreshed, with a more positive attitude and a general feeling of well-being. Things that had been bothering them may now be seen in a new and more helpful way. They have a different perspective on things and feel much more in control.

These reactions have been known for years, but only in recent times has a physiological explanation been available. Knowledge gained from brain scans and the measurement of brain wave patterns has given new information about the "alpha state".

When we are truly relaxed, both mentally and physically, there are changes in the brain wave pattern until it is predominantly within the alpha state. Within this state the brain triggers chemicals known as

Left: Mind and body work together in meditation to promote health and well-being in the whole person.

endorphins. It is this chemical trigger that has the benefits that are experienced as a feeling of well-being. Indeed, endorphins have been called "nature's own opiates". Meditation is one of the easiest ways to achieve this, and these good feelings can continue for some time after the meditation has ended, the length of time varying with each individual.

There is also a very real physical benefit, as these same endorphins also boost the immune system, thus helping the person to fight off infection and maintain good health.

Below: The change in brain wave patterns as a result of regular meditation can give you a feeling of alert calmness and increased mental composure. You may feel as if you are back in control again.

MEDITATION WITHIN THE CONTEXT OF A BUSY WORK LIFE

As mentioned earlier, the tensions of modern working practices often mean that people are so bound up in meeting all the demands placed upon them that they maintain a high level of mental and physical activity throughout their waking hours. This frequently means that they are not only cutting off their emotional responses and their enjoyment of the simple things in life, but are also pushing their physical and mental

health to the limit. Much has now been written about stress management, and the many books on the subject emphasize the need for a period of mental and physical relaxation at different stages in the day. They point out that by taking this time out one actually gains rather than loses when it comes to productivity, as the brain simply cannot maintain intense activity for long periods and remain efficient.

One writer, Ernest Rossi, has formulated the "20-minute rule", which is based on the theory of ultradian rhythms. Ultradian rhythms are biorhythms that the body works through during each day – a little like hyperbolic curves of energy which repeat every 90 to 120 minutes or so. Naturally, it would be best to work only at peak performance times, but this is just not possible. However, timing your work breaks to coincide with the mind/body slow-down pattern every 90 minutes ensures maximum productivity and restricts the build-up of stress.

Rossi suggested, and indeed practises, the pattern of working for 90 minutes and then taking a

Stress can become damaging when we can no longer control our responses to it.

20-minute break. He usually lies down and meditates in this period, as it is the best form of total mental and physical relaxation and good preparation for returning to optimum mental processing.

It is important that these breaks take place every 90 minutes or so, in such a way as to completely change the mind/body state. Ideally, you should stop all work activity and experience a change of physical status (standing rather than sitting, looking into the distance rather than close up, for example) and mental focus. A 20-minute meditation is ideal and the benefits will be felt immediately.

On returning to work after that 20 minutes, you will see things afresh and deal with them more quickly and efficiently, as the mind and body are alert and ready to climb up to peak performance again on the biorhythmic curve. The feeling of well-being will continue well into the next 90-minute period.

Is it coincidence that workers throughout the world have evolved breaks at approximately 90-minute intervals (coffee – lunch – tea)? This has grown up through experience, and has occurred in all types of work environment. Unfortunately, the intense demands of modern work practices, instant communication, and rising numbers of self-employed workers have meant that more and more people have found it convenient to take their breaks at the desk, or to ignore breaks altogether. It is a false economy, based on the premise that one can keep going indefinitely, and in fact, it leads to greater inefficiency and is harmful to both the worker and their work.

Left: Be aware of your biological clock throughout the working day and try to take a break every 90 minutes.

EXERCISES FOR PHYSICAL RELAXATION

The first essential in approaching the meditative state is to learn to relax fully. When you stop working, the tension that has built up in your mind and body remains and must be diffused before you can truly begin to benefit from a period of rest. A programme of exercises will loosen contracted muscles and make you feel refreshed, revitalized and physically relaxed. As well as unwinding the stresses in your body, exercise has the added benefit of releasing mental tension, so it can be a helpful prelude to every meditation session.

If strains and tensions are allowed to build up in the body they may lead on to a variety of aches and pains, as well as increasing mental strain and diminishing coor-dination and efficiency.

A single session of exercises for relaxation will immediately refresh and calm you. Loosening your muscles will also make you aware of areas of tension in your body, so that you can give some attention to sorting out the causes: improving your posture, the way you sit at your desk, or the shoes you wear.

Just as tension produces an arousal response, relaxation has the opposite effect on the body, reducing not only muscular tension but also rates of respiration and digestion, blood pressure and heart rate, while increasing the efficiency of the internal organs and the immune system.

While it is vital to relieve tension when you feel it building up into aching or stiffness, it is better to avoid such a build-up by incorporating relaxation exercises into your daily routine. Use them to stretch stiff muscles when you get up in the morning, or during a mid-morning or 20-minute afternoon break from work. At bed-time, taking a few minutes to release tension in your neck, back and shoulders will aid sound, relaxing sleep. Training your body to relax fully will calm your mind and prepare it for the meditative state.

Relax in a position that is comfortable for you.

RELAXATION EXERCISES FOR NECK, BACK AND SHOULDERS

1 Stand upright with your arms stretched above your head. Lift up on to your toes and stretch further still.

2 Drop forward, keeping your knees relaxed, and let your arms, head and shoulders hang heavy and loose for a while.

3 Shake out your head and arms, then slowly return to standing. Repeat a few times.

SITTING RELAXATION EXERCISES FOR NECK, BACK AND SHOULDERS

1 Sit upright in a firm chair with your lower back supported and your feet squarely on the floor, hip-width apart. Raise your arms above your head and stretch them upwards, feeling the pull in your upper body. Look upwards and hold the stretch.

2 Drop forward, letting your head and arms relax completely. Return to the starting position and repeat the exercise, staying aware of the changing tensions in the muscles.

3 To stretch the back, link your hands together over the top of the chair, and lift your arms slightly. Lean back gradually, arching your back over the chair, hold, then repeat.

ALTERNATE NOSTRIL BREATHING

1 Concentrating your attention on regular, quiet breathing is both physically calming and helps to clear your mind of any intrusive thoughts as an aid to meditation. Place the first two fingers of one hand on your forehead, with thumb and third finger reaching down on either side of your nose.

2 Relax your thumb and inhale through that nostril; pinch it closed again, then release the finger to exhale through the other nostril.

◀ **3** Breathe in on the same side, then close that nostril and breathe out on the other side. Continue to breathe slowly through alternate nostrils.

RHYTHMIC BREATHING
To most of us breathing is a totally mechanical act, but at times of stress we often breathe incorrectly. Practise these exercises to become aware of each breath and to help your breathing become more rhythmical and steady. Stop if you feel dizzy, and never force your breath.

POSTURES FOR MEDITATION

Meditation is a very personal experience and you can meditate anywhere that suits you – on the bus, along a beach, at home. It is important for you to find a position in which to meditate that feels comfortable for you. You should feel relaxed without drifting off to sleep, and you should be able to remain still for the period of meditation without experiencing any numbness or cramp in your limbs that would be distracting. Experiment with the following suggestions until you find what feels best for you.

SITTING ON THE FLOOR

Sit with your back straight and supported by the wall with your legs outstretched and feet together. Rest your hands on your thighs.

SITTING ON A CHAIR

Choose a firm chair that supports your lower back well. Put your feet together, resting flat on the floor, and rest your hands on your thighs. Keep your back straight but your shoulders relaxed, and your head up.

SITTING ON YOUR HEELS

This posture is a good one for your back as it keeps the spine straight. The feet should be relaxed with the toes pointing backwards. Use a cushion under your feet if you wish. Rest your hands lightly on your lap.

THE LOTUS POSITION

1 The half-lotus is the simpler version: bend one leg so that the foot rests on the opposite inner thigh. Place the second foot on top of the thigh of the first leg. Keep the spine upright and rest the hands lightly on the knees.

2 For the full lotus, the first leg should be bent with the foot on top of the other thigh, and the second leg then bent so that the foot goes over the other leg on to the opposite thigh.

LYING DOWN

Lie flat on your back with the whole of your spine in contact with the floor. Then relax your shoulders and neck. This position has the disadvantage that it may cause you to drift off to sleep.

Ways of Gaining the Meditative State
Sounds

Many religious groups, as well as adherents of Transcendental Meditation, talk of using a sound, or "mantra" to help with meditation, and indeed this can be helpful. The constant repetition of a phrase, a word or sound ("aum" is commonly used in Hinduism) creates the alpha state by an almost hypnotic focus of attention upon the sound. The Hare Krishna movement is well-known for its repetitive chant that is repeated over and over again, and can lead to its members seeming to become "high" – again the effects of endorphin release.

An effortless sound, repeated with the natural rhythm of breathing, can have the same soothing, mentally liberating effect as the constant natural sound of running water, rustling leaves or a beating heart. The single sound, or mantra as it is known, is used to blot out the "chatter" of intrusive thoughts, allowing the mind to find repose. Speaking or chanting a mantra as a stream of endless sound is a very ancient method of heightening a person's awareness by concentrating the senses. The simple gentle sound "om", or "aum", is sometimes known as the first mantra, which is literally an instrument of thought. The curving Sanskrit (the ancient language of Hindus in India) symbol for this primordial word represents the various states of consciousness: waking, dreaming, deep dreamless sleep and the transcendental state.

However, the sound need not be a special word, or incantation; something simple and meaningful will be as, if not more, effective. The sound of the word "calm" spoken or thought with each breath breathed out can be very, very effective, especially while imagining tension leaving your body and a calmness

The Sanskrit symbol that represents the sound "aum".

developing. The word "relax" seems to match other people's needs in a similar way. Any word that appeals to you will do, repeated with the flow of breath, silently in the mind, or out loud. This clears the mind, slows the breathing and allows relaxation, both mental and physical, to develop.

USING TOUCH

You can use your sense of touch in a lulling, soothing way to induce a state of meditation when you are under stress. Young children do this when they adopt a satisfyingly smooth ribbon or piece of fabric to hold and manipulate when they are feeling tense.

The same technique can commonly be seen all over the Middle East, where strings of worry beads are rhythmically passed through the fingers at difficult moments to focus the mind and calm anxiety. Their uniform size, gentle round shapes, smooth surfaces and rhythmic, orderly clicking as

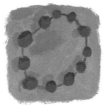

Worry beads.

they are passed along their string all assist the meditative state. Use one or two smooth, rounded stones in the same way, passing them from hand to hand, and concentrating on their temperature, shape and surfaces, or find an object with a tactile quality that particularly appeals to you.

The constant, yet variable sound of running water can be especially soothing.

COLOURS

Some colours are associated with relaxation and can be a helpful way to clear the mind of tension and allow meditation to start.

Sit with your eyes closed, and be aware of the colour that comes into your mind: it may be any colour of the rainbow – red or purple are common. Then slowly and gradually allow that colour to change to a blue or green colour, allowing it to fill the whole of your mind's eye and replacing all other colours. The colour pink is also recommended by colour therapists and this may prove helpful. You will find a feeling of relaxation growing as the new colour builds in your mind, and when the relaxed colour is complete, you will experience those pleasant feelings of inner peace and stillness associated with meditation.

BREATHING IN COLOUR

You can help the colour to build up by associating it with your breathing. Establish a comfortable rhythm of breathing and focus on it until your mind is clear. Allow your colour to fill your mind's eye, then, as you breathe in, imagine the colour filling your body, from the soles of your feet up to the top of your head.

Colours are associated with various qualities, so choose a colour to suit your individual needs. Red: vitality, energy, strength and willpower (complementary colour turquoise). Orange: happiness and laughter (complementary colour blue). Yellow: intellect and objectivity (complementary colour violet). Green: cleansing and harmony (complementary colour magenta). Turquoise: strengthens the immune system, counteracts disease (complementary colour red). Blue: peace and relaxation, restful sleep (complementary colour orange). Violet: beauty, dignity, self-respect (complementary colour yellow). Magenta: release of obsessional thoughts and memories (complementary colour green).

Make sure you are sitting comfortably – a cushion may help – and breathe in the colour of your choice.

COLOUR VISUALIZATION EXERCISE

Close your eyes and breathe calmly and regularly, focusing on the rhythm of your breathing. As you inhale, imagine that you are sitting on a beautiful lawn in a peaceful garden. Sense the cool freshness of the green stretching around you. As you breathe out, imagine the velvety magenta of a full-blown rose. Breathe in again and let the balanced, cleansing green fill your mind. Repeat a few times, then sit quietly for a few moments.

Below: Take in colour with each relaxed breath until the colours permeate your whole being and you feel immersed in colour.

Try to become aware of the wonderful colours of the natural world, such as in this field of lavender.

SIMPLE GUIDED PROGRAMMES

You may find it helpful to record the following meditation exercises on to tape, so that you can concentrate on gaining the images, or focusing attention, without worrying about forgetting a passage or having to refer to the page. When recording, just use your normal voice, speaking quite slowly but not drawing out the words in any unnatural way, speaking steadily and quietly, leaving pauses (indicated in the text by ". . .") to allow the mind to develop the image before moving on. You will soon find what feels comfortable for you. It is really very easy and leaves you free to enjoy the feelings and concentration that develops. It can be helpful to have some music in the background on the tape, or indeed while you do the exercises when you have committed them to memory, or when you have developed your own. When choosing music, select something non-intrusive and without sudden changes in speed or pitch.

PHYSICAL RELAXATION

Sit in a comfortable position, with your hands resting loosely in your lap or on the arms of the chair and your head balanced comfortably; let your eyes close and begin to relax.

First, think of the top of your own head, your scalp, and let all the muscles, skin and nerve-endings there . . . just relax and let go.

Thinking of your facial muscles, just tense them and scrunch them all up: around the eyes, the forehead, around the mouth, scowling and grimacing for a count of five seconds, then release and let go. Feel that relaxation in all those muscle groups; feel all the muscle groups beautifully relaxed and at ease. This may mean your mouth is slightly open, but choose whatever position is best and most comfortable for you . . . just allow it to happen. The more you physically relax the more you'll mentally relax too, so that soon . . . very soon, you can enjoy that pleasant feeling of half-sleep.

Thinking down through the neck and shoulder muscles . . . and on into the tops of your arms, allow

Sitting quietly and comfortably in your special place is a form of meditation.

those muscles to sag down, become tension-free. Thinking of the muscles of the upper arms, tense those muscles for a count of five and let them go, let them relax . . . down into the elbows and on to the forearms, just letting all those areas relax and let go. Down through the wrists . . . into the hands . . . clench your fists really tight for a count of five, then release, releasing any tension and leaving the hands and arms heavy, easy and relaxed.

Think for a moment about your breathing; you're breathing easily and evenly now, so you can let any tension in the chest area drain away, as you think down into the tummy muscles, letting them relax too.

Think down into all the muscles of your back and the muscles down either side of the spine. Allow those muscles to let go; relax and feel good . . . allowing the chair to take all the weight and all the strain.

Thinking into your waist . . . your hips . . . and down into your main thigh muscles, letting tensions drain down and away as you think down towards your knees . . . and on down into your shins and calves . . . allowing those muscles, too, to relax, feel comfortable . . . and let go as you think on into the ankles and down into the feet, into the toes, right the way down to the very tips of the toes . . . All your muscles are relaxed, tension-free and feeling good.

Tense your facial muscles – feel the tension around your eyes and mouth – then let it go.

Clench your fists – feel the tension in your fingers, hands and arms – then let it go.

THE NUMBERS GAME – A MEDITATION FOR ADULTS OR CHILDREN

This is a very simple meditation using a blackboard, real or imaginary. It is a good "game" to use with children, to give them an experience of meditation: they really enjoy it. It is presented as if you are leading a group of children, but it can be easily used by an adult, and is an excellent way to clear the mind through concentration, imagination and patterns, all of which are wonderful ways of gaining a real experience of deep meditation.

1 Get the children to sit or lie comfortably. Once they have found a really comfortable position ask them to remember it, and then sit up, knowing they are going to return to this relaxed position in a few moments.

2 With chalk on the blackboard, draw a diagram of numbers, three lines by three columns, making sure that there are no mathematical links, like this:

```
3  1  5
8  6  9
4  7  2
```

3 Give the children one minute, and really show them that you are timing it, to memorize this pattern in lines and columns. They will be working with this later in their mind's eye (that screen on the inside of the forehead).

4 Ask them to return to their relaxed position, eyes closed. Ask them to concentrate on the numbers, and if anything else comes into their mind, to recognize it and then push it away (repeat this often during the session).

5 Rub out lines or columns of numbers, telling the children what you are doing and asking them to do the same in their mind's own diagram . . . do this slowly. Keep the pace of your speech slow too . . . give time for them to adjust, and tell them what is left as a check, for example, "That leaves just four numbers". Continue until they reach the last number. Really concentrate on that number . . . long pause . . .

6 Then rub out the last number, saying "Now concentrate on what is left" . . . Let them remain in silence until you notice a restlessness – this is often three or more minutes.

7 Wake them gently, by speaking in a soft voice becoming louder with an instruction to "Sit up". Ask them what the last number was and for their reactions.

THE HAVEN – YOUR OWN SPECIAL PLACE

Once you have managed to achieve complete physical relaxation and calm,
allow your mind to enter a place, whether real or imaginary,
that is special to you.

Now you can allow your mind to drift . . . drift to a pleasant, peaceful place. A place that you know and where you always feel able to relax . . . completely. A safe . . . secure . . . place . . . where no one . . . and nothing can ever bother you.

It may be a place you have visited on holiday, a beach or a place in the countryside. Or it may be a room . . . a room you have had . . . a room you do have . . . or a room you would like to have . . . an imaginary place. But it is a place where you can always feel able to let go . . . completely . . . a haven, a haven of tranquillity, unique and special to you.

A time and a place, real or imaginary, that is your special meditative place.

In order to help you imagine this place . . . notice first the light: is it bright, natural or dim . . . is there any particular source of light . . . natural or man-made? Notice also the temperature level . . . hot, warm or cool . . . and any particular source of heat. Be aware of the colours that surround you . . . shapes . . . and textures . . . the familiar objects that make that place special.

You can just be there . . . whether sitting, lying or reclining, enjoying the sounds . . . the smells . . . the atmosphere . . . with nobody wanting anything, nobody needing anything and no one expecting or demanding anything from you . . . you can truly relax.

A Guided Visit to a Country House

Imagine that you are visiting a beautiful country house . . . a really beautiful old country house or stately home, on a warm, sunny, summer's afternoon. You are standing on the staircase that leads down into the entrance hall, one of those wide ceremonial types of staircase. And as you look down across the entrance hall, you can just glimpse, through the open doors opposite, a gravel drive, and the sunlight on the gravel. It's a beautiful, sunny, summer's afternoon and there is no one around to trouble or bother you as you stand on that staircase . . .

Now you are moving down the last ten steps to the hallway, relaxing more and more with each step down.

10 Taking one step down, relaxing and letting go . . .

9 Taking another step down, feeling at ease . . .

8 Becoming more relaxed, letting go even more . . .

7 Just drifting deeper . . . and deeper . . . and even deeper down still . . .

6 Becoming calmer . . . and calmer . . . even calmer still . . .

5 Continuing to relax, continuing to let go and feeling good . . .

4 Relaxing even more . . . letting go even more . . .

3 Sinking deeper . . . drifting even further into this welcoming, relaxed state . . .

Walk steadily down the path, aware of the colour, scents and sounds that surround you.

2 Enjoying those good feelings, feelings of inner peace and relaxation . . .
1 Nearly all the way down now, feeling very good . . . beautifully relaxed . . . and **0**.

You are wandering across that hallway now, towards the open doors and the gardens beyond, soaking up the atmosphere of peace and permanence in that lovely old building.

You wander out through the doors and down the stone steps outside . . . and find yourself standing on the gravel drive outside, a wide gravel drive that leads down to the entrance gates.

As you stand there you notice the lush green lawns, so flat and well-clipped . . . and there are shrubs and trees, different shades of green and brown against a clear, blue sky . . . and you can feel the warmth of the sun on your head and shoulders as you enjoy this beautiful summer's afternoon in this lovely old garden. . . . There are flowerbeds with their splashes of colour

so carefully arranged and neatly tended. And there's no one else about . . . nobody needing anything, nobody wanting anything and nobody expecting anything from you, so you can enjoy the peace and serenity and solitude of this afternoon in this beautiful garden that's been so well looked after for so many, many years.

A little way down on the right-hand side of the driveway, you notice an ornamental fish pond, the sort of fish pond you only find in the grounds of an old country house or stately home. So you decide to wander down and have a look at those fish, and begin to scrunch your way down that gravel drive, with nothing disturbing the peace and stillness of that afternoon but the scrunch of the gravel as it moves beneath your feet, and the occasional bird song from a long way away, emphasizing the stillness of the air. You are wandering down towards the fish pond, soaking up the atmosphere of this beautiful garden full of flowers and butterflies.

Eventually . . . eventually you find yourself standing near the edge of the fish pond, looking down into that clear, cool, shallow water, just watching those fish . . . large ornamental goldfish of red and gold, black and silver, swimming so easily . . . gliding so effortlessly among the weed, in and out of shadows and around the lily pads. Sometimes they seem almost to disappear behind the weed and shadows, but always they reappear, with their scales catching the sunlight, red, gold, silver or black.

And as you watch those fish your mind becomes even more deeply relaxed . . .

THE WELL

This continues from the previous visualization of the country house and is intended to take you to even deeper levels of meditation. Alternatively, you can use it just on its own to focus the mind beautifully.

. . . As you watch those fish you notice that the centre of the pond is very, very deep, it could be the top of a disused well.

You take from your pocket a silver-coloured coin, and with great care toss that coin so that it lands over the very centre of the pond, and then you watch as it swings down through the water. The ripples drift out to the edges of the pond, but you just watch that coin as it drifts and sinks deeper and deeper through that cool, clear water, twisting and turning; sometimes it seems to disappear as it turns on edge, at other times a face of the coin catches the sunlight and it flashes through the water . . . sinking, drifting deeper and deeper, twisting and turning as it makes its way down . . . Finally it comes to rest at the bottom of the pond, lying on a cushion of soft brown mud, a silver coin in that still, clean water on its own cushion of mud . . .

And you feel as still and undisturbed as that coin, as still and as cool and motionless as that water, enjoying that feeling of inner peace and stillness.

Watch the spreading ripples as the coin lands in the very centre of the pond.

SUGGESTED MEDITATIONS
A STONE OR ROCK

Once you have gained those relaxed feelings associated with meditation, you can use this time by focusing your attention in various ways. You may meditate on an object, for example, in order to gain insights and self-knowledge. Almost any object can be used, but natural ones seem to be most popular.

Its shape, colour and texture . . . age . . . hardness . . . warm . . . cold . . . wet . . . dry . . . weathering . . . gradual change . . . earth . . . mountain . . . boulder . . . rock . . . pebble . . . gravel . . . sand . . . time . . . change . . . adaptation . . . response . . . but always there . . . permanence . . . "you are my rock".

Above: It might be the shape, texture or colour of the rock that appeals, but it is important to choose a rock or stone that feels right for you.

Right: A single piece of rock might be best for meditation, but consider, too, rocks of all shapes and sizes, perhaps in a stream.

A FLOWER

Choose a flower and place it in front of you. Use your chosen technique to obtain inner attention, then open your eyes and focus upon the flower. You may find a flow of thought developing, or a collection of words building in your mind. Here are examples of each of these ways of meditating, but please remember that your mind can work in many ways, and should be allowed to flow naturally rather than being directed to match this interpretation.

A flower, in full bloom, the colour in the petals, the connection to the stalk, the way each petal is formed, and the differences and similarities there. How natural and beautiful, the shading and subtle changes caused by the light . . . This flower is at its peak of perfection . . . soon the petals will open and then fall . . . a seed pod will develop there . . . the seeds will scatter . . . some will find earth in which to rest and in the natural cycle of things will stay dormant . . . until the time is right . . . The light and temperature trigger new growth . . . a tiny shoot will then develop and grow, emerging from the soil . . . larger leaves will unfold, then a stalk carrying a tiny green bud will emerge, and as this swells through the casing, colours will emerge and the flower bud will emerge . . . This will develop and form into another flower just like this one, and light and shade will allow its true beauty to be enjoyed again.

Natural beauty . . . colour . . . light . . . shade . . . perpetual change . . . the seasons . . . death . . . decay . . . rebirth . . . growth . . . perfection . . . the natural cycle of living things.

Right: Natural perfection is transitory, but is wonderful in its form, colour and beauty.

Above: Focus on an imaginary exotic flower. Below: The natural cycle of birth, growth, death and rebirth.

A flickering candle flame, with its ever-changing light that gives colour, shape and form to all it illuminates, is one of the most popular images to focus on during a meditation session.

A CLOCK TICKING

The hands of a clock record the passage of time – time never stands still although our perception of time can change. Past – present – future, the clock registers the moments of life moving forward. Focusing on a clock image can be very restful.

The clock ticks . . . the hands move . . . so slowly . . . always moving . . . seconds tick away . . . The one just passed is over . . . a new one takes its place . . . it too is replaced . . . as time moves on . . . Each moment lasts only a second . . . The clock may stop . . . time . . . never stops, it moves on . . . The moment that is over is out of reach . . . the moment to come has not arrived, yet . . . this moment is MINE . . . this moment I can use as I wish . . . I focus on this moment . . . I influence this moment . . . I can use this moment . . . and no other NOW!

Measurement . . . movement . . . monitoring . . . invention . . . mechanism . . . complexity . . . regularity . . . cogs . . . gears . . . chains . . . weights . . . pendulum . . . interaction . . . perpetual motion . . . never still . . . always moving . . . key . . . battery heart.

Hold an image of a clock face in your mind and imagine the hands slowly moving around the face.

A PICTURE

This can be a way of bringing the outside world into your meditation, or coming to an understanding of another person's view of the world. Select a picture, religious or otherwise, and having gained a meditative state, allow yourself to focus that acute attention upon the picture and let your thoughts flow. They may be about the total picture, or one aspect of it, or the making of the picture and what was intended by its creator. Let your mind do the work for you, and you can be sure that it will be utilizing the picture to stimulate insights that are helpful and relevant to your needs at that moment.

A picture tells a story – the story as depicted by the artist or photographer, the story as seen and interpreted by the world of the viewer. One picture can tell many stories – all different – all are the interpretations of the viewer's mind at the moment of viewing.

USING THE MEDITATIVE STATE
LEAVING TROUBLES BEHIND

This meditation, which is known as the "railway tunnel", is particularly helpful
in leaving troubles behind, gaining perspective and focusing on the here and now,
uncluttered by past concerns.

Imagine yourself strolling along a very straight flat path. It's a dull, cloudy, drizzly sort of day, the path is leading between two high banks, there is damp grass beneath your feet, and you can see the cloudy sky above. Somehow you feel heavy, you are aware of a heavy back-pack on your shoulders, making your steps heavy and slow. Your back is bent a little to support the weight and you seem to be looking at the ground in front of you as you trudge along the path, feeling damp and cold and weighed down. You glance up and see the entrance to an old railway tunnel: this must be a dis-used railway line. As you look, you

can see a point of light at the other end of the tunnel, so it cannot be too long. You decide to continue on your walk; at least you will be out of the drizzle in there. As you approach the entrance, the tunnel seems very dark, but that small circle of light at the far end is reassuring so you keep moving forward into the tunnel

. . . At first it seems very dark, you can hardly see at all, but the floor feels even and it is easy to walk along. As you do so, all those old doubts about yourself begin to surface in your mind; you are aware of your own failings and those things you wish you hadn't done, and indeed the things you wish you had done in the past . . . Just let them come gently to the surface of your mind. The back-pack seems to be getting a little lighter as these different doubts and regrets unpack from your inner mind, gently and easily. You keep walking, and notice a pool of light on the floor ahead . . . there must be an air shaft there. As you go through the pool of light you suddenly remember a happy time, when someone really enjoyed your company, a time when you felt really good about being you. As you move out of the light into the darkness again you feel lighter still, the back-pack is emptying and you are standing a little straighter now, but the doubts are rising to the surface, the regrets are floating up into your mind again. The circle of light at the end of the tunnel is getting bigger now, but here is another air shaft, with that shaft of light penetrating the gloom of the tunnel. Again, as you pass through that light, another good memory of being appreciated for who you are, being praised for something, or complimented, comes to the forefront of your mind. Now you are back in the gloom, but it doesn't seem as intense as before. It is getting lighter and warmer step by step now, and more and more good memories of those who have loved you and events that pleased you come into your mind . . . As you get nearer to the end of the tunnel you notice that the sun must be shining because it all looks very bright out there, and you find that you feel so much lighter, as if you have lost that back-pack altogether now, and a pleasant warmth is beginning to replace any traces of damp and cold that you felt before.

Eventually you step out into the bright summer sunshine, and smell the aroma of freshly cut grass, and walk out with a light tread into the warmth of a

Focus on the fluidity of clouds as they slowly disperse.

bright summer's day, feeling lighter and valuing yourself and the world around you much more. You realize you have still so many opportunities and possibilities awaiting you and new chances to do things that make you feel good about yourself, and at ease with others. Your contribution is important, and you are a valuable and lovable human being.

Walk out of the tunnel into a brighter, lighter world.

MEDITATION FOR PERSONAL DEVELOPMENT AND GROWTH AFFIRMATIONS

Affirmations are a deceptively simple device that can be used by anyone and have proved remarkably effective. You should try to use this method while in the meditative state, having previously planned and memorized the affirmations involved. Thus, you combine ease of communication with all parts of the mind and the effectiveness of repeated powerful positive phrases. The technique requires you to say to yourself, out loud, a positive statement about yourself as you wish to be: examples are given later.

To make affirmations effective, they should
• be made in the present tense
• be positively phrased
• have an emotional reward.
If you notice what happens if you are asked not to think of elephants, you will realize why negatives (the words "no", "not", "never" and so on) will have the opposite effect to that intended. Yours is the most influential voice in your life, because you believe it! Be aware of any negative statements you regularly make about yourself, either to others or to yourself – "I am shy," "I lack confidence," "I cannot," "I get nervous when" and so on – they are self-limiting beliefs that you are reinforcing each time they slip into your conversation or mind. Now you can use affirmations while meditating to change those beliefs.

Right: Affirmations change the way you think about yourself and the way you act and react.

VISUALIZATION

In the same way that you can utilize your voice, so, perhaps more powerfully, you can use your imagination. The imagination can stimulate emotions, and these can register new attitudes in the mind. It can be a direct communication with the deeper levels of the mind and can provide a powerful influence for improvements in your attitudes, behaviour patterns and overall confidence.

Visualization requires that you imagine yourself in a situation, behaving, reacting and looking as you would wish to do at an interview, an important meeting, a social gathering, a one-to-one situation, or perhaps a sporting event. Imagine what that will mean for you, your reactions, the reactions of those around you and, importantly, feel all the good feelings that will be there when this happens in reality.

It is like playing a video of the event, on that screen on the inside of the forehead, the mind's eye, from the beginning of the situation through to the perfect outcome for you. Should any doubts or negative images creep into your "video", push them away and replace them with positive ones. Keep this realistic, and base it upon real information from your past. Once you are happy with the images you are seeing, note the way you are standing and

presenting yourself. Then allow yourself to "climb aboard", and view the scene from inside your imagined self. Now you can get in touch with the feelings and attitudes that make the event successful. The best time to do this is when relaxed mentally and physically – during meditation. Teach yourself to expect new, positive outcomes. This can be combined with affirmations, to make it doubly effective.

Rehearse the forthcoming event in your mind's eye so that you are fully prepared.

IMPROVED SELF WORTH

We all have attributes and qualities in which we can take pride and pleasure.
This exercise is about emphasizing these positive aspects to allay the doubts that
only serve to limit our potential.

• I like my [physical attribute]
• I am proud of my [attitude or achievement]
• I love meeting people – they are fascinating
• My contribution is valuable to [name person]
• I am lovable and can give love
• Others appreciate my [opinions, assistance, a personal quality]
• I enjoy being a unique combination of mind and body

Imagine yourself speaking to colleagues, boss, employees or friends . . . See yourself behaving and looking confident, standing and looking a confident person . . . Notice how you stand . . . your facial expression . . . hear the way that you speak . . . slowly, calmly, quietly, clearly and with

Right: Value yourself and acknowledge your own positive features and qualities.

See yourself in different situations: at home, in a social setting, in all the parts of your life, being a confident, self-assured person. You are valuing your own talents, and the inner strengths that come from experience . . . knowledge . . . skills . . . insights . . . understanding . . . attitudes . . . patterns of behaviour . . . strengths that support you in everything you do.

Above: Be aware of how you stand, your facial expressions and the feelings involved.

confidence. You are communicating your needs . . . ideas . . . opinions in a positive way. Notice how your words flow easily, and how others are listening attentively to you . . . valuing what you have to say. Now "climb aboard" . . . be there – know how it feels to stand like that . . . to speak like that . . . and to have that positive reception from others. Get in touch with the stance . . . expression . . . and feelings . . . and know that you can use these any time in the future to gain those same feelings or inner strength supporting you in everything you do.

Above: Always try to be open with others so that they feel able to be open with you.

FOR INSTANT RELAXATION

Having trained yourself to meditate and to gain those feelings of focused attention combined with physical relaxation, you can utilize the "triggers" you have been using to gain the same feeling of relaxation at any time. If you have been imagining being in a certain place, doing so will instantly give you those feelings, or if you have been using a trigger word the same is true.

It may be that you are aware of certain physical symptoms during meditation, such as a tingling in the hands or feet: this too may be a useful trigger. Imagine that you feel those symptoms and you will gain the sensations and feelings associated with meditation within seconds. This can be especially useful before an important meeting, or any occasion about which you may be feeling a little apprehensive, in order to gain the calm confidence you need and to put things into their proper perspective.

Your mind has accepted the training and linkages you have created during meditation, and will respond to the same signals or triggers at any time, quickly and easily, for all the benefits that come with the practice of meditation.

Left: Meditation is excellent for recharging the batteries and rediscovering vitality, energy and well-being.
Right: A tropical beach with all its beauty, warmth and tranquillity provides a lovely mental image to focus on during meditation.

FOR CONFIDENCE IN FUTURE SITUATIONS

The meditative state, affirmations and visualization can be a valuable rehearsal and preparation for a future event. Athletes and other sports people have proved that it works. We can all use this process to achieve our own optimum performance in any situation.

• I am quietly confident in meetings
• I speak slowly, quietly and confidently so that others listen
• My contribution is wanted and valued by others
• I enjoy meetings, as they bring forth new ideas and renew my enthusiasm

Imagine a meeting that is about to happen, and see yourself there, filling in all the details that you know, and the people too; imagine yourself there looking confident and relaxed, concentrating on what is happening. Be aware of the acute interest you are giving to what is happening, complete, concentrated attention, and then imagine yourself speaking, to give information or to ask a question: hear yourself speaking quietly, slowly and calmly . . . Notice people listening to what you are saying; they wish you well and support you, as you are expressing your viewpoint or raising a question they may well have wanted to ask, too. Notice how you are sitting or standing, how you lean slightly forward when speaking . . . that expression of calm confidence on your face. When this is clear in your mind, just like a film playing in your mind's eye, play it back and forth. When you are feeling comfortable with it, get into that imaginary you, "climb aboard" and be there in your mind, seeing things from that perspective, hearing things from that point in the meeting. As you speak, get in touch with those calm feelings, and the attitudes that allow you to feel calm, in control, and quietly confident there . . . It is like a rehearsal; the more you rehearse the better the final performance will be. You will acquire the attitudes, stance and tone of voice, so that when you are in that situation all of these will be available to you, and it will be just as you imagined, as if you had done it all, successfully, before.

Imagine yourself at an important event where you are at ease.

The moment of initial introductions can be tense, but remember how you looked, stood and felt in your visualization.

The preparation was worth it, having given your best and feeling good about your performance.

FOR LIVING FOR NOW

Although we cannot change the past, we can learn from it and build up skills and useful insights from it. The future is that unknown world of possibilities and opportunities before us – but all that we can truly have any effect upon is now.

- I have learned a great deal from the past
- The future is an exciting range of opportunities
- I am able to enjoy my acute awareness of this moment
- I am living NOW

- NOW is the beginning of the rest of my life
- I enjoy laying good foundations NOW on which to build a better future

Imagine yourself standing on a pathway, a pathway that stretches in front of you, and, if you look over your shoulder, trails behind you, the way you have come . . . As you look around, you are aware that the area immediately around you, to the left, right and above, is brilliantly illuminated, and that sounds are amazingly clear. You are acutely aware of all that is happening around you, and your reactions to it. Now that you look ahead again, you see that the path in front is there, but is dim in comparison with the area around you. As you check over your shoulder you notice the path behind is even less clear. You hear a clock chime in the distance and take a step forward, and strangely that bright, acute awareness immediately around you travels with you . . . You notice the slightest of noises, movements or shifts of light, and take pleasure even in the pure sound of silence, too. You can hear

The past is over, the future is unknown and so the only time we can truly affect is NOW.

For a complete experience, be more acutely aware of shapes and textures as well as sounds, colours and scents.

that same clock ticking now, and with each tick you can take a small step forward, effortlessly, along the path, and that illumination and awareness moves with you, so that you are constantly acutely aware of the here and now . . . At any fork in the path you can make decisions easily and quickly, as you are truly involved in the moment, rather than looking over your shoulder at what might have been, or staring blindly into the future at what might happen. You enjoy being in the brilliantly illuminated, acute awareness of sound, hearing, feeling, taste and smell that is NOW.

Appreciate the qualities of your food: its colour, shape and aroma, its temperature, texture and flavour.

FOR HEALTH

The mind and body are so completely interlinked that if we keep physically fit
we are also mentally alert. Likewise, if we utilize our mental capacities we can affect our
physical health and performance, too.

• I feel safe in the knowledge that my body is constantly renewing itself
• It feels good to know that every damaged cell is replaced with a healthy one
• My immune system is strong and fights off any infections easily
• My mind and my body are working in harmony to keep me healthy

Imagine yourself lying or sitting comfortably. As you see yourself there you notice a healing glow of coloured light surrounding your body, but not touching it. Let that colour become stronger, until it has a very clear pure colour, the colour of healing for you.

Now, as you watch, that healing, coloured light begins to flow into the top of your head. You can see it slowly draining into all parts of the head, face, ears, and

Meditation can help free you of physical tension and mental anxiety.

starts its journey down through the neck and shoulders, into the tops of the arms . . . It continues to flow down through the arms and the chest area, that healing, coloured light, penetrating all the muscles and organs . . . even as you watch you can also feel a healing warmth coming into your body . . . NOW . . . as it flows down into the stomach area, the back, right the way down to the base of the spine. At the same time it is reaching your fingertips too, and that warmth is there in your body right now . . . It continues to flow down through the legs towards the knees, down into the calves and shins, the ankles and on into the feet. All the way into the toes, that healing, coloured light just glows throughout the whole body now.
And now that the whole body is suffused with

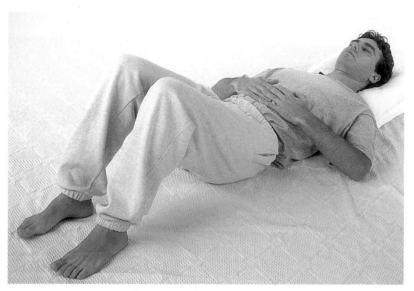

Concentrate on areas of the body that need healing, and imagine yourself free of aches, pains, illness and tension.

Exercise promotes physical fitness and improves mental clarity.

coloured, healing light, and there is a warmth throughout your body, you notice the light concentrating in certain areas, areas that need healing attention. The warmth there seems more obvious as that healing light focuses upon repairing and replacing damaged tissue and focuses your own inner resources to help and heal and bring comfort to that area.

And you feel that area gaining the benefits of that healing light, combined with comfortable warmth. Then you can allow the light to disperse again and gradually return to your normal wakeful state, knowing that in those areas that need it, the healing process will continue to focus your own healing resources into the necessary repair and replacement cycle that is so natural and normal in all living creatures.

Health is a combination of the mind and body.

FOR DECISION MAKING

If there are alternatives to be considered and a decision to be made, you have an inner adviser who can be helpful. We all have a higher self, made up of a conscience and an ideal self towards which we strive. It is not always possible to get in touch with this important resource while going about our daily business, but when in meditation, in that inner stillness, those inner resources become available.

It may help to imagine your inner advisor as a wise old man or woman, or a bird such as the wise owl.

Some may wish to imagine sitting in front of a wise old man or woman – this may be an image of someone we have known in our life, or a completely imaginary being. Some may choose an animal or a bird, such as an owl, as the focus of attention. Having imagined this inner adviser in whichever way suits you, now imagine being with that adviser and asking a simple question about your problem, then wait . . . You may get a very real insight straight away, or it may be that your adviser uses a present or gives you a scene to think about, or may even open up a possibility not yet considered. At first the answer may seem obscure, but at some later point the meaning will become obvious to you.

We all have an inner adviser, a source of wisdom, formed perhaps before birth, but constantly being brought up to date by our day-to-day experience of the world around us, and our own reactions to it. It is a valuable resource, and with the help of meditation you can use it to give you the confidence to make decisions, and move forward into your future.

Right: You may like to imagine a friend as your inner advisor. Below: Different cultures have adopted particular animals as symbols of wisdom.

FOR REDUCTION OF STRESS

Stress is a factor in everyone's life and can even be a major motivator in some circumstances. Meditation can be a great help in coping with it, and combined with visualization, it can change your whole response to the many stressful demands of modern living.

• I enjoy solving problems
• I work well under pressure
• I am a calm, methodical and efficient worker
• I love that feeling of having achieved so much in a day
• I enjoy being calm when others around me are not

Imagine yourself in a situation that has in the past caused stress. Picture the situation, and the other people involved . . . See yourself there . . . and notice a slight shimmer of light between yourself and those other people . . . a sort of bubble around you . . . a protective bubble that reflects any negative feelings back to them . . . leaving you able to get on with your tasks . . . your life, with an inner strength and calmness that surprises even you. A protective, invisible bubble surrounds you at all times. It will only allow those feelings that are positive and helpful to you to pass through for you to enjoy and build upon. Others may catch stress from each other . . . negativity, too, can be infectious . . . but you are protected . . . you continue to keep things in perspective . . . and to deal with things calmly and methodically. You are able to see the way forward clearly . . . solve problems . . . find ways around difficulties . . . by using your own inner resources and strengths, born of experience.

Now see yourself talking to someone who has been causing pressure to build. Find yourself knowing just how to let them know that what they are doing, or saying, is unhelpful in resolving the problem or difficulty. Find yourself able to let them know in such a way that they can accept without offence . . . and find your own calmness and control . . . a strength that supports you. You can let someone know if too much is being expected, and explain why. See yourself in that situation . . . calmly explaining the areas of difficulty . . . being able to supply examples and information until they understand the position. At all times you are surrounded by that protective bubble of light that keeps you calm and quietly confident, thinking everything through clearly and explaining it simply to others.

Next, imagine pushing out through that same protective bubble emotions that are unhelpful . . . past resentments . . . and hurts . . . embarrassments, too. You push them out through the bubble . . . where they can no longer limit or harm you. You are now better able to control the way you feel and react . . . The bubble stays with you and enables you to remain in control . . . keeping things in perspective . . . having the strength to change those things you can change . . . accept those things that you cannot . . . and move on!

Left: Your protective bubble will stay with you always whatever you do. Right: Always try to see things how they really are rather than allowing problems or difficulties to be distorted or magnified by worry.

FOR IMPROVED CONCENTRATION AND STUDY SKILLS

The pressures that are experienced when studying for an examination can actually disrupt concentration and so one's ability to learn and remember information. Meditation in this visual form can re-energize the ability to learn.

• I enjoy those moments of insight and understanding
• I enjoy using my mind and expanding the boundaries of my knowledge
• My memory is expanding with new information
• My learning ability improves with use
• I concentrate so completely that nothing but an emergency can distract me

Imagine a huge jigsaw spread out in front of you: it is a giant picture made up of many smaller images, and each image is a jigsaw in itself. Some images are nearly complete, others are only just starting to form, some even seem a confused jumble of unattached pieces. Focus your attention on one image, just one part of the giant jigsaw, one that is nearly complete but is still a little confusing – you are still not quite sure what the image will turn out to be.

A new piece comes into your hand, and you see that it fits, it fills a gap as it interlocks with all the surrounding pieces . . . The image suddenly becomes clear, and you can see it now. You have a wonderful feeling of achievement, for something that was unclear is now clear; that which was confusing is now fully understood. You feel just as you do when a new piece of information interlocks with other information and you understand the whole subject. That insight . . . that moment of learning . . . the joy of understanding is what makes learning so worthwhile.

Should you ever need to retrieve that piece of the jigsaw, to answer a question of some kind, you know . . . you know that it is there . . . and all the interlocking pieces that together give insight and understanding are all there all the time for you to select and use when you need them.

The memory is like a giant jigsaw, and the moments of achievement when understanding and enlightenment take place are the joy of learning itself.

As you enjoy learning, so you enjoy total concentration as you study, take notes and engross yourself in the process of learning. It is, for that study period, as if nothing else matters but exercising your intelligence in the process of gaining information, skills and insight, and expanding the capabilities of your mind. Only an extreme emergency could distract you. Learning is a continuous part of being alive.

FOR GOAL ACHIEVEMENT

A goal, in all areas of life, is important in order to focus one's attention
and inner resources. A goal provides a sense of direction and
ultimately the joy of achievement.

• I direct my energies to achieve my goals
• I enjoy directing my energies positively
• I know where I am going and how I am getting there
• Step by step I am moving in the right direction
• I have the ability, I have the determination, I shall succeed

Be aware of the different areas of your life; work, social, leisure activities, emotional and spiritual. Select one of these for this exercise . . . and be aware of what you want to happen in that area of your life, what you want to achieve . . . Make it realistic and clear in your mind. It may be useful to write it down, and describe it fully before beginning this visualization.

While in the meditative state, imagine yourself having achieved that goal, imagine yourself there, in that situation. Surround yourself with all the things or people that indicate that you have achieved that goal. Be as specific as you can . . . be aware of all the senses . . . what are you seeing . . . hearing . . . touching or sensing . . . smelling . . . tasting. Be there . . . make it real . . . be specific . . . about colours . . . temperatures . . . lighting, to make it more and more real in your mind.

Be there and know how it feels to have achieved that goal . . . Be aware of how it makes you feel . . . how it affects your mood . . . and your feeling about yourself.

Now, from where you are at that moment of achieving that goal . . . look back . . . as if along a path, a pathway of time . . . to where you were . . . and notice the different stages of change . . . of movement towards achieving that goal . . . along the way . . . along that path . . . the different actions you have taken . . . the contacts you have made . . . and the people involved. Be aware of the smallest moments of change that have happened from where you were to this moment of having achieved your goal . . . from the start of the journey to its fulfilment . . . Be aware of all the stages along the way . . . and as you return to the here and now . . . you remain in touch with the feelings that will make it all worthwhile . . . and you feel more and more determined to take one step at a time . . . make one change at a time . . . along that path to the successful achievement of your goal.

And as you return from the meditative state . . . as you return to full wakefulness . . . so you are more and more determined to be successful in the achievement of your goal and to take the first step towards it, today.

Below and left: One step at a time and eventually you will reach your goal and enjoy the view and the feeling of success.

FOR IMPROVED CREATIVITY

Many adults have a craving to be creative but underestimate their ability to be so. Creativity takes many forms and everyone is creative in some way or another. Use these exercises to rediscover your latent creativity and rebuild your confidence in your skills and talents.

• I enjoy my own creativity
• I am blessed with a vivid imagination
• I love to express myself in creative ways
• I enjoy my own imaginative responses to the world as I see and feel it

Imagine yourself in a wonderful room . . . a room surrounded by windows looking out on to countryside . . . In this room there are many small areas, and you can move freely around the room trying each of the areas to see how you feel . . . Here on the left is a large piece of paper with pens and pencils, a small studio for drawing and sketching . . . Another area has an easel and paints set out ready for you, the artist, to take up . . . Another has clay for you to handle and form into shapes or pots . . . Another has a word processor ready for your fingers to create images in poetry or prose . . . Yet another has many engineering tools for the inventor . . . Another has cameras and photographic equipment . . . Just spend some time moving around and trying them all . . . these are just some of the areas into which you may choose to channel your own creativity, and where no one else need judge or approve. Only your opinion matters, and the joy of translating the inner world of the imagination into a form or expression that suits you . . . Which feels most stimulating, most exciting, and most comfortable?

Become more and more aware that everyone has a creative ability, to tell stories, to create beauty, to capture a moment . . . Imagine yourself using one of the

Inspiration can come in many forms: natural or man-made; real or imaginary.

Left: There are so many different ways to express one's creativity. Below: Children are naturally creative and that creativity remains with us into adulthood. It is there within us just waiting to be rekindled.

areas in this marvellous room, or indeed finding another area not yet described . . . in order to create your response to the world around you, or your inner world. Be aware of the feeling of having time and energy to channel into this creative activity. Be aware of the focus of attention that this creates for you; nothing else seems to matter . . . but the ability to utilize your innate creativity . . . and the joy that comes when something tangible forms in front of you. For many the process is more exciting than the end product – which gives you the greater satisfaction?

Sometimes we drive smoothly and happily along a road, we come to traffic lights on red and have to pause. The creative flow can be like that too, but the lights turn to amber and then green and off we go, just as you will when that temporary block dissolves . . . Enjoy your creativity and imaginative power, and translate it into the world around you. You know that you can do it, for your own sake, for its sake, free of the need to please anyone else but yourself.

BALANCE AND STRENGTH: *Yoga Stretching*

HAVE YOU EVER WATCHED A CAT WAKING UP? More often than not, it will give an exaggerated yawn, then arch its back until stretched to its limit, before loosely letting go and gracefully moving off on its way. Have you ever stopped to wonder why it makes these movements? The cat instinctively knows the value of stretching to maintain flexibility and improve circulation to the muscles; you too can become stronger and more flexible with regular yoga stretching.

PREPARATION

One of the best things about stretches is that you can do some simple exercises anywhere, at any time: at home, in the office, standing in a queue or even sitting in the car. However, in order to get the most benefit from regular stretching, and particularly yoga practice, it is important to create a quiet, comfortable space and to give yourself the time to do the movements without pressure or interruptions. Making this space, both literally and in the busy schedule of the day, is in itself a relaxing, unwinding step and will enhance the effectiveness of the actual exercises.

Ideally, make an area that feels quiet and calming to you, perhaps with softer lighting if it is needed at all, maybe with a mat for the stretches and postures for which you need to lie down. If you have any back discomfort, or just need extra support when lying down, then a couple of cushions may be useful. It is helpful to wear loose clothing so that you can move freely and easily. If the weather permits try to let in some fresh air – but do not get cold: these exercises are not intended to work up a sweat or strain the heart, but to make you less stiff and tense, and generally more flexible.

To assist in creating a smooth, flowing movement, become conscious of your breathing while you are doing the exercises. This helps you to feel fully involved in the movements, anticipates stress and offers a sense of harmony in linking breath, body and mind. Except when resting, always breathe through your nostrils rather than your mouth, co-ordinating the speed of the movement with the speed of your breath. Forward bending movements are generally done with an exhalation, backward bending movements with an inhalation.

Yoga exercises are best learnt in a class with an experienced teacher; for maximum benefit, however, a regular practice time between classes is important. The following exercises are mainly stretches that you can do on your own, for self-help with relaxation. If you become inspired to take up more of these postures, do find a good, local class – and also create a little environment at home in which you can enjoy yoga stretching regularly. You may find that your partner, family or friends want to stretch with you; use these exercises to release tensions, improve circulation, tone your body and have fun as you stretch.

CAUTION:

The stretching exercises suggested in this book are intended as a general guide to movements for increasing flexibility, improving muscle tone and circulation, and helping to maintain good posture. Clearly, they are not a substitute for individual advice or good yoga or exercise classes, and if you are in any doubt about how to do an exercise, or whether it is suitable for you, seek advice from a qualified teacher.

If you have any physical health problems, such as a back injury, or suffer from a medical condition that gives rise to worry about doing any of the stretches, you should seek medical advice. For some conditions, such as high blood pressure or thyroid problems, inverted postures such as the "Plough" are contra-indicated.

If you have not done any exercise for a while, start stretching gently and build up your flexibility gradually. Easing out tension through stretching can make muscles ache at first, but none of these exercises should be painful: stop if there is acute discomfort. In the main, you should feel only benefit from including some yoga stretching in your daily life, becoming more energized, supple and improving your posture. It's always wise to remember, however, if in doubt, don't do it.

WARM-UP EXERCISES

Before starting to do any serious stretching, it is important to do some warm-up exercises.
They will ensure that your muscles are warmed and loosened and will help to prevent any strain.
These gentle exercises can also be carried out on their own at any time if you are feeling stiff.

SHRUGGING SHOULDERS

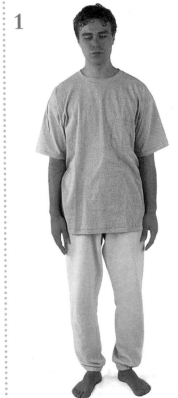

1

▲ Stand upright with your feet slightly apart and your shoulders relaxed.

2

▲ Lift your shoulders up as high as they will go, then let them fall down again. Repeat a few times.

ARM CIRCLING

1

▲ Wheel your arms around from the shoulders in slow, large circles.

SQUATS

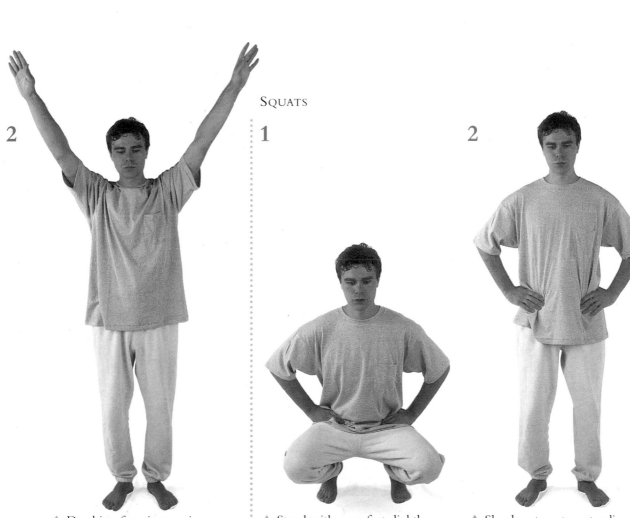

2

▲ Do this a few times going backwards, then repeat circling your arms forwards.

1

▲ Stand with your feet slightly apart, hands on hips. Go slowly down into a squatting position.

2

▲ Slowly return to a standing position, then repeat, always trying to keep your back upright.

LOOSE TWISTS

1

◀ In a standing position with feet comfortably apart and knees relaxed, swing your arms loosely backwards and forwards around your body.

▶ Keep your head and body facing forward all the time and keep your feet and pelvis still. Repeat a few times to loosen your arms and shoulders.

2

ARM-STRETCH BREATHING

1

▲ Stand with your arms straight out in front of you, at chest height. Take in a deep breath.

2

▲ As you inhale, move your arms out to the sides, keeping them raised. As you exhale, bring your arms back to the front. Repeat three or four times only.

CAT STRETCH

1

▲ Kneel on all fours, with your hands and knees shoulder-width apart. As you inhale, bring your head forward and slightly hollow the back.

2

▲ Now breathe out and, as you do so, arch the back upwards like a cat, allowing your head to drop down. Repeat a few times.

SIDEWAYS BEND

1

▲ Stand with your feet at least shoulder-width apart and your arms at your sides. Bend down to one side, trying not to twist.

2

▲ Slowly return to the upright and then bend to the other side. Straighten and repeat.

SHAKE

▲ Try to relax and let your whole body go completely floppy. Shake your limbs to release any tension.

79

FLEXIBILITY ENHANCERS

Stretching is not only important to encourage blood to flow back into tense, contracted muscles, but it also helps to increase suppleness and to relieve stress. When performing exercises to maintain flexible joints, you should aim to balance the movements: any forward bending of the spine, for instance, should be matched by following it with a backward bend movement.

FORWARD BEND

1

▲ Stand with your feet apart and knees slightly bent.

2

▲ Breathe in, lean forward and grasp your legs: try to hold your ankles if you can reach.

3

▲ Exhale, and as you do so straighten your legs; on breathing in let the knees flex again. Repeat.

THE BOW

1

▲ Lie on your stomach, arms down by your sides and knees bent.

2

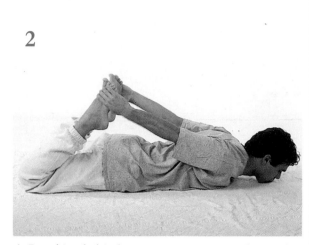

▲ Reaching behind you, try to grasp your feet with your hands.

3

▲ Lift your head and feet as far as is comfortable, and hold for a moment or two. Relax your body slowly to the floor and repeat twice.

CAUTION:
Some of the movements described are fairly challenging if you have not done any regular exercise for a while. You may find that to begin with you are not sufficiently flexible to achieve the final posture. Do not overdo or strain to do any of these movements; allow your body to lengthen and loosen gradually with regular practice.

THE PLOUGH

1

▲ Lie down on your back, with arms down by your sides and your hands flat on the floor for support. Raise your legs in the air.

> CAUTION:
> Like the Bow posture, this yoga position may be too difficult for some people, so do not strain too hard in trying to achieve the final position.

2

▲ Keep your legs going over your body towards your head as your bottom lifts off the floor.

3

▲ If possible, let your feet touch the floor behind your head.

4

▲ To return, flex your legs before letting your body come back over into the original position.

CHEST EXPANSION SEATED

This movement opens up the chest muscles and helps the flexibility of the spine.

1

2

▲ Sit in a cross-legged position, and clasp your hands together behind your back, raising your arms as far as is comfortable. To stretch the chest muscles further, breathe in as you raise your arms, then relax them slightly as you exhale.

▲ Inhale, then as you breathe out bend forward, your arms staying as high as possible to maintain the stretch. Uncurl your body slowly and return to the upright sitting position. With continued practice, you may be able to bring your arms into the vertical position. As with all stretches, never strain.

HEADACHE AND TENSION RELIEVERS

Many of us suffer from tension headaches and know that they begin with a feeling of pressure in the head or neck, or a taut sensation in the facial muscles. A few simple stretches can help to relieve this muscular tension and prevent it leading on to a severe headache. They can be done almost anywhere.

SIDEWAYS NECK STRETCH

1

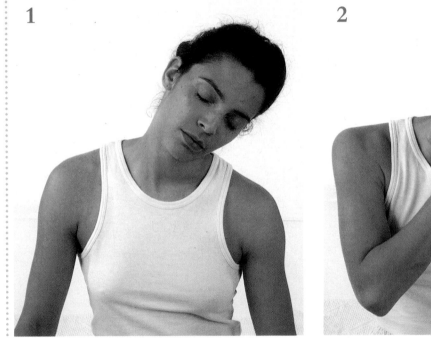

▲ Slowly stretch your head down to one side, feeling the pull in the neck muscles. Return the head to the upright position and repeat on the other side.

2

▲ To make this stretch of the neck muscles more effective, use your hands to give extra leverage. Place one hand under your chin and the other on top of your head; as you stretch sideways exert a steady pressure with both hands to add to the movement. Change hands and repeat on the other side.

HEAD TO CHEST

▲ Lower your head towards your chest, feeling the pull on the back of the neck. Hold at your furthest stretch before slowly raising the head again. Repeat two or three times.

LION POSTURE

▲ To stretch the facial muscles and release tension, open your mouth as wide as possible and push out your tongue. At the same time, open your eyes into as wide a stare as you can manage. Hold for a moment or two, then relax. Repeat a couple of times.

SEMICIRCLE ROTATION

1

▲ Turn the head to one side, then steadily rotate it in a semicircular movement, letting the chin drop down across the chest.

2

▲ Dropping the head backwards compresses the neck, so it is best not to make this a full circle rotation. Repeat, going back in the opposite direction.

SHOULDER TENSION
RELIEVER

1

2

▲ In a kneeling position, interlink your fingers and raise your arms above your head.

▲ Stretch up as far as is comfortable and hold for a moment. Repeat three times.

POSTURE ENHANCERS

One of the benefits of an exercise system such as yoga is the increase in grace and poise that comes from improving your posture. Holding yourself properly can help you to look and feel younger, and reduce muscle strain. Try these stretches to help you regain your natural postural integrity.

STANDING TWIST

1 **2**

▲ Stand with feet slightly apart and arms raised straight out in front of you. Slowly twist your body to one side, keeping your feet firmly steady on the floor.

▲ Return to the centre and repeat on the other side. You can gain added benefit by keeping your feet together and rising up on to tip-toe before twisting.

RISHI'S POSTURE

1

2

3

▲ Stand with your feet shoulder-width apart, and hold your arms out in front of you.

▲ Bend over, sliding one hand down the inside of the same leg, while the other arm points up.

▲ Reach as far as is comfortable, then slowly return to the upright and repeat on the other side.

TREE

1

2

ARM AND LEG STRETCH

▲ Stand on one leg and bend the other knee, raising the foot so that it rests on the inner thigh of the supporting leg. Raise the arms and hold the stretch, then repeat with the other leg.

▲ You can either place your palms together above your head, or raise the hands aloft.

▲ Stand on one leg and bend the other leg up behind you. Grasp the foot with the same hand and raise the other arm to point to the sky. Pull up on the foot and stretch up with the raised arm. Hold the stretch, then repeat with the other leg and arm.

TENSION AND BACKACHE RELIEVERS

The most common cause of lost time at work is backache. In the great majority of cases, back trouble is the result of chronic tensions, which build up in the back region. Tired, tight muscles are also much more prone to strain or injury. The stretches that we show here are intended to aid flexibility of the spine, but if you already suffer from back pain or an injury, seek professional advice.

COBRA

1

▲ Lie on your front, with your arms bent so that your hands are under your shoulders, palms facing down.

2

▲ Slowly lift your head and push down on your arms to help raise your trunk. Exhale as you raise your body.

3

▲ If you can, tilt your head backwards and stretch up and back as far as possible. Hold briefly, then relax and lower your body back down. Repeat.

BOTTOM RAISE

1

▲ Lie on your back with your knees bent and feet flat on the floor, arms down by your sides.

2

▲ Push up with your bottom, lifting it and holding at the furthest limit. Lower, relax and repeat.

> CAUTION:
> Some of these stretches are quite difficult yoga postures: never force any movements or try to stretch too far.

SIMPLE TWIST

1

▲ Sit on the floor with your legs straight out in front of you.

2

▲ Bend one leg and place the foot on the floor across the other knee.

3

▲ With your opposite arm, reach around the bent leg to catch hold of the straight leg, then twist your body. Relax and repeat on the other side.

FULL TWIST

1

▲ If you find the previous movement fairly easy, try to get a little more leverage on your lower spine by bending one leg so that the foot is resting on the inner thigh of the other leg.

2

▲ Bring this leg over the first one, then grasp your foot with the other arm.

3

▲ Twist as far around as you find comfortable, hold, then relax. Swop over your legs and repeat twisting to the other side.

BENDING TWIST

▶ Stand with your feet shoulder-width apart and your arms straight out to the sides.

▶ Bending forward, try to touch your foot, or the floor in front of it if you can, with your opposite hand. Slowly uncurl and return to the starting position. Repeat on the other side.

TRIANGLE

▲ Stand with your feet shoulder-width apart and your arms stretched out to the sides.

▲ Bend down to one side without twisting your body, letting the opposite arm rise in the air.

▲ Stretch the raised arm, look up and hold. Slowly straighten and repeat on the other side.

SLOUCH STRETCH

1

▲ Sit on a tall stool so that your feet are off the floor. Hands behind your back, slouch so that your back is rounded, with your head lowered towards your chest.

2

▲ Flex one foot, and lift the leg to straighten it if possible. Release the leg, relax, then repeat a few times. Repeat with the other leg.

LOCUST

1

▲ Lie on your stomach, with your arms down by your sides and your feet together.

2

▲ Keeping your upper body on the floor, try to raise both legs off the floor together, keeping them as straight as is comfortable. Lower the legs, relax for a moment and repeat. Do not strain too hard to have perfectly straight legs; as you become more supple this will be easier to achieve.

CHEST HUG

1

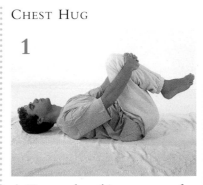

▲ To complete this sequence of exercises, relieve any strain in the back by lying on your back with legs bent up and hands clasped around the knees.

2

▲ Lift your head and hug your legs into your chest, hold, then relax. Take care not to strain your neck when lifting your head.

BREATHING AND BLOOD FLOW ENHANCERS

Chronic tensions and anxiety can often make us feel very tight across the chest, so that it becomes difficult to breathe deeply. To improve breathing and blood flow to the chest muscles and lungs, use these stretching exercises on a regular basis. Expanding the chest enables the lungs to fill with more oxygen, which will, in turn, nourish all the cells in the body, including the respiratory organs themselves.

COMPLETE BREATH

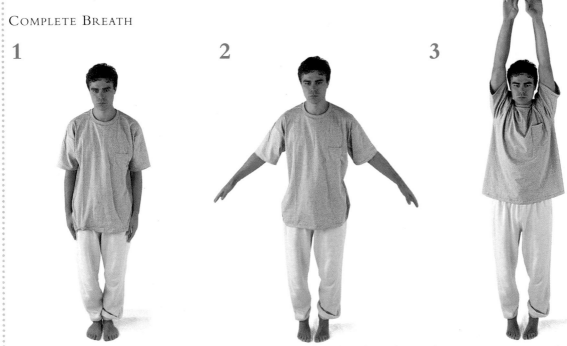

1

▲ Stand with feet together, arms by your sides.

2

▲ Slowly take a deep breath, and as you do so raise your arms out to the side.

3

▲ Raise your arms until they meet over your head, and at the same time rise up on to your toes. As you exhale, slowly return to the original position. Repeat this exercise two or three times only.

BACKWARDS BEND, KNEELING

1

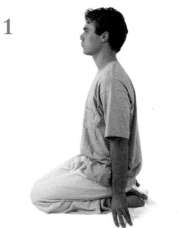

▲ Kneel on the floor, sitting on your heels. Place your hands on the floor just behind you.

2

▲ Raise your trunk to arch up and back as you inhale. Hold for a moment, then sink back into the kneeling position as you exhale.

BACKWARDS BEND, STANDING

▲ Stand with hands on hips. Breathe in, then exhale as you bend backwards from the waist. Avoid if you have back problems.

CHEST EXPANSION

1

▲ Stand with feet together and clasp your hands together behind your back.

2

▲ Try to raise your arms a little, leaning back slightly. Then lean forwards as far as possible.

3

▲ Keep your arms lifted as high as is comfortable. Slowly straighten up, relax and repeat.

TIRED AND ACHING LEG REVIVERS

Standing or sitting, most of us spend too long each day with our legs stuck in fixed positions. Stiffness of the lower limbs from inactivity or tension can make us feel generally tired. Legs benefit greatly from being stretched, keeping them toned and supple. These exercises will prevent the legs, thighs and lower back from getting too tense, and help you to move freely.

ALTERNATE LEG PULLS

1

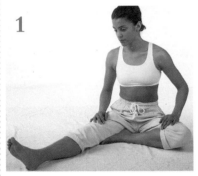

◀ Sit on the floor, with one leg out straight and the other bent so that the foot rests on the inner thigh of the extended leg.

▶ Lean forward and clasp the straight leg as far down as is comfortable; pull your chest down a little further and hold for a moment. Change legs and repeat.

2

FULL LEG PULLS

1

▲ The previous stretch can be extended by starting with both legs straight out in front of you.

2

▲ Lean forward and hold the legs with both hands; pull yourself down a little further and hold for a moment. If this is difficult, bend the legs slightly.

Side Leg Raise

◀ Lie on your side with your legs and body in a straight line. Support your head with one hand and place your free hand on the floor in front of you for balance.

◀ Without twisting your hips, steadily raise the upper leg as far as is comfortable. Hold, then lower slowly. Repeat with the other leg.

Cat Stretch

▲ Kneel on all fours with your hands and knees shoulder-width apart. Raise your head and look straight ahead.

▲ Breathe in, and as you exhale lift and arch your back. Hold for a moment before relaxing back into the original position. Inhale, then repeat.

KNEE AND THIGH STRETCH

▲ Sit on the floor and bend your legs so that the soles of your feet are together. Hold the feet with your hands and try to pull the feet a little closer to your body. Let the knees drop down towards the floor, hold the stretch, then bring up your knees to relax. Repeat.

LEG OVER

1

▲ Lie on your back, with legs out straight. Raise one leg as close to the vertical as is comfortable, then move it across the body, keeping your hips on the floor.

2

▲ Allow the leg to go as far over as possible, then slowly return to the original position. Repeat with the other leg.

▼ CAUTION: Do not strain yourself with this movement – it works on lots of muscles at the same time.

BACK PUSH-UP

1

▲ Lie on your back with your knees bent and your feet on the floor, hip-width apart. Place your hands on the floor by your shoulders.

2

▲ Push up with your hands and feet, arching your back at the same time. Hold for a moment, then lower your body back to the floor.

SIT UP/LIE DOWN

1

▲ Sit on the floor with both legs straight out in front of you.

2

▲ Slowly lower your back to the floor, then start to bend the legs and raise them off the floor.

3

▲ As you raise the legs, straighten them until they are as close to the vertical as possible.

4

▲ Keeping the legs straight, slowly lower them to the floor.

5

▲ Continue the movement by sitting up and clasping your legs with your hands to bend forwards. Slowly return to the original sitting position.

TENSION AND POOR CIRCULATION

When our legs and arms become very tired, either through general tension or muscle fatigue, the contraction of the muscles can lead to poor circulation to the extremities. This can become a vicious cycle, as the restricted blood flow fails to nourish the muscles adequately, leading them to stay in a more contracted state. One or two simple stretches can help to restore blood supply to the area as well as relieving tight, cramped muscles.

CALF STRETCH

▲ Sit on the floor with one leg out in front of you; if possible, lean forward and grasp the foot with your hand. Pull the foot gently towards you, feeling the tightness in the calf. If you are unable to hold the foot in this position, try doing this stretch with the leg slightly bent. Repeat with the other leg.

▶ Stand upright and lift one leg off the floor. Clasp your hands behind the knee to pull the leg towards your chest. Relax, then repeat with the other leg.

HAMSTRING STRETCH

CALF AND FOOT EXERCISE

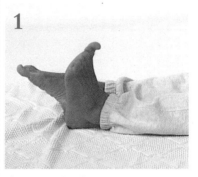

1

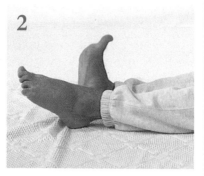

2

▲ Sit on the floor with both legs straight out in front of you, then alternately flex and extend each foot.

▲ You should have one foot flexed while the other is extended, and vice versa.

FINGER PULLS

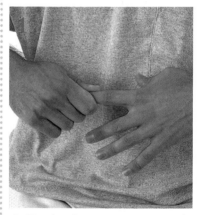

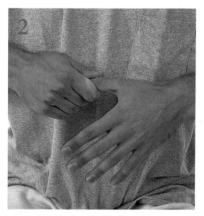

▲ Hands often store tension and feel tight: to help ease out tension, take one finger of one hand and grasp it firmly with the other hand. Give it a steady pull.

▲ Repeat for each finger in turn. Then swap hands and repeat.

THIGH STRETCH

▲ The muscles in the front of the thighs, the quadriceps, can be stretched by standing on one leg and bending the other leg up behind you. Clasp the foot with your hand and pull it further up towards the back. Hold, then relax. Repeat with the other leg.

REVITALIZING PASSIVE STRETCHES

One of the nicest and most effective ways to ease out really tired, tense muscles after a stressful day at work is by means of passive stretching. In these exercises, someone else helps your body to extend and stretch that little bit further. Assisting with these revitalizing stretches can be a very positive way to help your partner unwind and release any stored tension. They can do it for you next time you are tired and tense.

HEAD TO CHEST

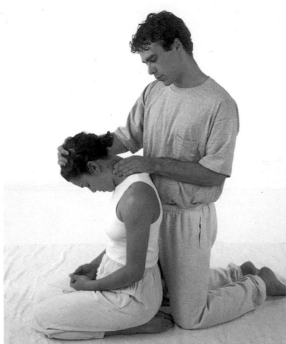

▲ With your partner kneeling up, place one hand on the back of the neck. As your partner lowers his/her head towards the chest, use your other hand to give added resistance by pulling down on the neck muscles.

NECK TRACTION

▲ Ask your partner to lie down, and sit or kneel at his/her head. Cradle the head in your hands and gently pull towards you to stretch the neck.

CAUTION:
Do not over-stretch the neck, and avoid this exercise if your partner has any injury or discomfort in the neck joints (for which they should seek professional advice).

ARM PULLS

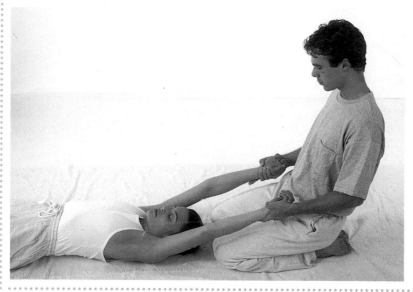

◀ With your partner lying down, take both wrists in your hands and bring the arms over the head. Steadily pull towards you, but do not cause discomfort or pain in the shoulder joint. Hold briefly and repeat.

LEG PULLS

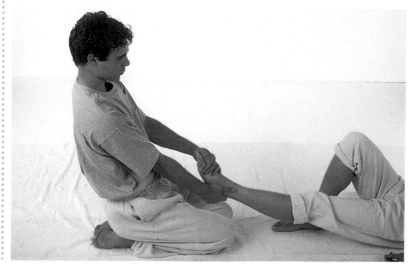

◀ Finally, with your partner lying down take one ankle in your hands and give a steady pull with the leg slightly raised off the floor. Hold and repeat, then do the same to the other leg.

INSTANT FATIGUE REVITALIZERS

Chronic stress and tension can easily lead to fatigue and exhaustion. If you find that your memory and concentration seem to be worse than usual and that stress leads to constant tiredness, then you may find these exercises, which aim to improve circulation to the brain, helpful.

SHOULDER STAND

1

▲ Lie on your back, with your legs straight and your arms by your sides. Raise your legs until they are vertical. Continue to lift your legs over your head while raising your bottom off the floor.

2

▲ Support your lower back with your hands and slowly try to bring your back and legs to the vertical position: do not strain.

3

▲ Hold for a few moments, then return in the same way to the original position.

> CAUTION:
> Do not do any exercises which involve an inverted posture if you have high blood pressure or an over-active thyroid gland, without first seeking medical advice.

FISH POSTURE

1

2

◀ Lie flat on your back.

◀ Arch your back until the top of your head is resting on the floor. Hold, then relax.

LEG CLASP

1

2

▲ Stand upright with your feet together. Bending forward, clasp your hands behind your legs, as far down as is comfortable.

▲ Steadily pull your head towards your legs. Go only as far as you can without strain. Hold for a few moments. Then slowly uncurl and return to the upright.

BACKWARDS BEND, STANDING

▲ Stand with your hands on your hips, feet slightly apart. Breathe in, then exhale as you bend backwards from the waist. Do not go further than is comfortable, and avoid this stretch if you suffer from back problems.

RISHI'S POSTURE

▲ Stand with your feet shoulder-width apart, and your arms raised in front of you.

▲ Twist your body and bend over so that one hand slides down the inside of the same leg, while the other arm points up to the sky.

▲ Look up at the raised arm. Reach as far down the leg as is comfortable, then slowly return to an upright position and repeat, bending the other way.

SIMPLE STRETCH

◀ Place several cushions or a low stool on the floor and lie on your back so that the cushions support you in the lumbar area, with your head lower than your pelvis. Relax in this position. Using a stool will raise your bottom higher, and even more blood will flow back to the brain. Make sure that there is no strain on your back.

DOG POSE

1

▲ Stand with your feet slightly apart, then place your hands on the floor, as far in front of you as you can manage comfortably.

2

▲ Try to straighten your legs. As you do so, arch your back, stretching up into an inverted V shape; hold for a while, relax and repeat.

CHILD'S POSE

◄ Finally, rest and relax your body by kneeling on the floor and bending forward to place your head on the floor, with your arms down by your side. This position can be relaxing after any back bends.

> ### CAUTION:
> If you have suffered a back injury, seek medical advice before doing these stretches. Always stop any exercise immediately if you feel acute discomfort.

ACCUMULATIVE STRESS RELIEVER

During long hours working at a keyboard or gazing at a monitor screen it is easy to adopt a slumped or hunched posture, while a long period of immobility can easily lead to tension and pain around your neck and shoulders. It's important to take short breaks at regular intervals to minimize the build-up of tension in these areas and to prevent the onset of a tension headache. Use this exercise while at your desk or during a break to alleviate any symptoms.

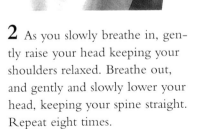

1 Sit with your feet apart and your spine erect, your hands on your thighs. With eyes closed, imagine focusing on a point on the floor. Maintain this internal focus for a few minutes.

2 As you slowly breathe in, gently raise your head keeping your shoulders relaxed. Breathe out, and gently and slowly lower your head, keeping your spine straight. Repeat eight times.

3 Breathe in slowly and raise one hand to touch your forehead, while at the same time raising your head. As you breathe out, lower your hand and head. Repeat eight times, alternating hands.

4 Now raise both hands together as you breathe in and lower both as you breathe out. Repeat this sequence eight times.

5 Resting your hands on your thighs, turn your head from side to side with each breath: as you breathe out, turn your head to the left; as you breathe in, bring it back to the centre. Repeat, turning to the right. Repeat this sequence eight times.

6 Take a breath and, as you exhale, raise your hands, bringing your palms over your eyes. Breathe once, then as you breathe in again return your hands to your thighs. Repeat four times.

7 Lie on the floor, let your breathing settle and your body soften. Focus your attention on any tightness in your body and use your outward breath to release it. Continue for two minutes, then rest for a minute.

ABDOMINAL TENSION RELIEVERS

We tend to hold much of our tension in our abdomen, especially if we bottle up feelings. Even simple muscular tension can leave us less flexible around the waist; exercises to reduce stiffness and increase flexibility in the abdominal region are useful in many situations.

SIDEWAYS BENDS

1

▲ Stand with feet apart and hands on hips. Bend down to one side, trying not to twist at the same time.

2

▲ Slowly return to the upright position and then bend to the other side. Repeat a few times.

ROLL TWIST

1

2

3

▲ Stand with feet apart and hands on hips. Keeping the legs and hips still, roll your upper body around in a clockwise circle.

▲ Move slowly and bend only as far as is comfortable.

▲ Repeat the roll in the opposite direction.

ABDOMINAL MOVEMENTS

1

◄ Either sit cross-legged or kneel, and place your hands on your waist or thighs. Breathe out completely.

► Without inhaling, pull in your abdomen as far as you can, then "snap" it in and out up to five times before taking a breath. Relax for a few moments, breathing freely, before repeating.

2

LEG OVER

1

◀ Lie on your back, with legs out straight. Raise one leg as close to the vertical as is comfortable, then move it across the body, keeping your hips on the floor.

▶ Push the leg as far over as possible, then slowly return to the original position. Repeat with the other leg.

2

LYING TWISTS

▲ Lie on your back with your hands behind your head and legs together, knees slightly bent.

▲ Twist the legs from one side to the other, keeping as much of the back and hips on the floor as possible.

Sit Up/Lie Down

1

▲ Sit on the floor with both legs straight out in front of you.

2

▲ Slowly lie back down, then start to bend the legs and raise them off the floor.

3

▲ As you raise the legs, straighten them until they are as close to the vertical as possible. Hold, then, keeping the legs straight, slowly lower them to the floor.

4

▲ To finish the sequence, sit up, and then bend forwards, clasping your legs with your hands. Slowly return to the original sitting position.

OFFICE TENSIONS AND STIFF MUSCLES

For people who spend their working day sitting at a desk, whether at home or in an office, it is very easy to get stiff and aching muscles. As we get tired, so our posture suffers and we can find ourselves becoming round-shouldered. Many office chairs are not good for the posture, and long hours spent staring at a computer screen can give our neck, upper and lumbar back muscles a very hard time. Regular breaks help: get up and walk around every now and then, and also try to loosen your body using some of these simple stretches while sitting at your desk.

ARM AND BACK STRETCH

▲ Link your hands together, palms away from your body, and push your arms straight out in front of you. Hold for a couple of moments, relax and repeat.

ARM AND CHEST STRETCH

▲ Link your hands together behind your back, over the top of the chair, and lift your arms slightly. Push away from your body, hold, then repeat.

FOREARM STRETCH

▲ Take your arms straight out to the sides and stretch them out.

▲ Alternately flex and extend your hands. Feel the pull on the upper and lower sides of your forearms as you do so.

BACK AND SHOULDER STRETCH

▲ Stretch your arms up in the air over your head. As you take a breath, arch your back slightly. Relax with the exhalation and repeat a couple of times.

POSTURE CLASP

▲ Take one arm behind your back and bend it upwards, with the hand reaching towards the opposite shoulder. With your other arm raised and bent downwards over your shoulder, try to clasp your fingers, or even your hands, together. Hold for a short time, then repeat with your hands in the opposite positions.

SEATED CAT STRETCH

1

▲ Pull the chair back from the desk slightly to give yourself more room, then bend forward and clasp your ankles.

2

▲ Arch your back to stretch, relax and repeat.

CALF STRETCH

▲ Sit fairly upright, then lift and straighten each leg alternately.

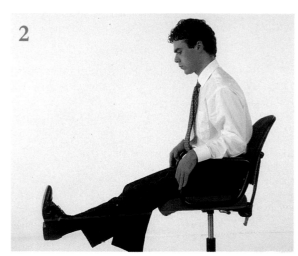

▲ Flex the foot to stretch the calf muscle. Repeat a few times.

NECK TWISTS

▲ Slowly turn your head to one side, feeling the extension in the neck muscles.

▲ Repeat, turning the head from side to side.

SHOULDER RELEASE

▲ Finally, link your fingers together and stretch your arms high above your head.

WAKING-UP STRETCHES

Do you wake up feeling stiff and tired, maybe even still a little tense from the stresses of yesterday? A few simple stretches can make you feel more refreshed, and better able to face a new morning. Stretching gets the blood flowing, bringing oxygen to your body's cells, and helps you to wake up.

COMPLETE BREATH

1

▲ Stand with feet together, arms down and head bowed.

2

▲ Slowly take a deep breath, and as you do so lift your arms out to the side and raise your head. For a more extended stretch, rise up on to your toes.

3

▲ Keep raising your arms until they meet over your head, and at the same time rise up on to your toes. As you exhale, slowly return to the original position. Repeat two or three times only.

FORWARD–BACKWARD BEND

1

2

▲ Stand with your feet slightly apart and your hands on your hips. As you inhale, bend back from the waist.

▲ Now exhale, bending forward as you do so. Slowly return to the upright, relax and repeat, holding each stretch.

STANDING TWIST

1

▲ Stand with your feet shoulder-width apart and arms straight out to the sides.

2

▲ Twist from the waist to one side, then twist around to the other side. Make the movements slowly and freely.

CAT STRETCH

1

2

3

▲ Kneel on the floor and curl up into a ball.

▲ Now move out on to all fours, hollowing your back slightly as you inhale.

▲ As you exhale, arch your back, hold and relax. Return to the original position and repeat.

TRAVELLERS' STRETCHES

If your work involves a lot of travel, whether by car, train or plane, you will be uncomfortably aware of how stiff you can feel at the end of the day. Long journeys place quite a strain on our bodies, and we can arrive tired, tense and fatigued even aside from any mental strain which may accompany the trip. If the journey is going to take several hours, try to take frequent short breaks. Doing some simple stretching exercises during or shortly after a journey can relieve tensions and refresh both body and mind.

SIDEWAYS BENDS

1

2

HAMSTRING STRETCH

▲ Stand with feet shoulder-width apart, arms outstretched. Bend down to one side, trying not to twist the body.

▲ Slowly return to the upright position and then bend to the other side. Straighten and repeat.

▲ Stand upright and lift one leg. Clasp your knee, then pull the leg up towards your chest. Relax, then repeat with the other leg.

THIGH STRETCH

▲ Bend one leg up behind you. Clasp the foot and pull it further up towards the lower back. Feel the stretch on the thigh. Relax and repeat with the other leg.

FORWARD–BACKWARD BEND

1 ▲ Stand with your feet slightly apart, hands on your hips. As you inhale, bend back from the waist.

2 ▲ Bend forward as you exhale. Slowly return to the upright, relax and repeat, holding each stretch.

BACKWARDS BEND

▶ Stand with your hands on your hips, feet slightly apart. Breathe in, then exhale as you bend backwards from the waist. Return to the upright as you breathe in.

CAUTION:
Do not go further than is comfortable, and avoid this stretch if you have back problems. After a journey, you can be quite stiff and it may be beneficial to shake your whole body before starting.

HIP AND PELVIC TENSION

The pelvic basin is an important area in the body, containing the reproductive organs as well as the bladder and the lower part of the bowel. Stretching exercises can benefit this region; they help to improve blood flow to and from the area and tone all these organs. The shape of the pelvic structure means that blood can pool in this area, and the stretches suggested here can relieve congestion, among other things helping to ease period pains or aiding better prostate function.

SIT-UPS

1

▲ Lie on your back with your legs bent, feet apart, and your hands behind your head. Breathe in.

2

▲ As you exhale, lift your head off the floor as far as is comfortable; hold for a moment, then relax. Repeat.

TWISTING SIT-UPS

1

▲ Lie on your back as before. Inhale, then as you breathe out raise your head and twist, at the same time raising your leg so that opposite elbow and knee move towards each other.

2

▲ Relax, then repeat, twisting the other way.

PARTIAL TWIST

1

▲ Sit on the floor with your legs straight out in front of you.

2

▲ Bend one leg, and place the foot across the other leg.

3

▲ With your other arm reach around the bent leg to catch hold of the straight leg, then twist your body as illustrated. Relax and repeat on the other side.

KNEE AND THIGH STRETCH

▲ Sitting on the floor, bend the legs so that the soles of the feet are together. Hold the feet with your hands, and try to pull them a little closer to your body. Let the knees drop down towards the floor, hold the stretch, relax and repeat.

BUTTERFLY POSTURE

▲ The knee and thigh stretch can also be done while lying down. Lie on your back and bend your legs so that the soles of the feet are together. Allow the knees to sink towards the floor and hold for several moments. This can be useful during pregnancy, and by stimulating blood flow it can also help men with prostate problems.

BOTTOM RAISE

◀ Lie on your back with your knees bent and feet flat on the floor. Put your arms down by your sides for support.

▶ Push up with your bottom, lifting it off the floor and holding at the furthest limit. Lower, relax and repeat.

SHOULDER STAND

▲ Lie on your back, with your legs straight. Raise your legs until they are vertical, then continue to lift them towards your head while raising your bottom off the floor. Support your lower back with your hands.

▲ Try to bring your back and legs to the vertical position, but do not strain. Hold for a few moments, then return in the same way to the original position.

CHEST HUG

▲ At the end of these exercises, relieve any strain in the lumbar area by lying on your back with legs bent up, hands clasped around the knees. Lift your head and hug your knees into your chest, hold and relax.

WINDING-DOWN STRETCHES

At the end of a long day it can be easy to fall into bed with many muscles still being held tight and contracted and the mental stresses of the day's work weighing on your mind; this can lead to disturbed sleep, or worse still you may not even be able to get to sleep. To help your mind and body release the day's tensions and prepare for a sound night's sleep, spend a few quiet minutes doing these winding-down stretching exercises.

NECK STRETCH

▲ Slowly stretch your head down to one side, feeling the pull in the neck muscles. Return the head to the upright position and repeat on the other side. Move slowly and hold each stretch for a moment.

LION POSTURE

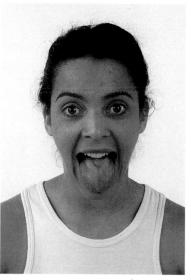

▲ To stretch the facial muscles and release tension, open your mouth as wide as possible and push out your tongue. At the same time, open your eyes into as wide a stare as you can manage. Hold for a moment or two, then relax. Repeat a couple of times.

FORWARD BEND

▲ Stand with feet apart and knees slightly bent. Lean forward and let your arms hang freely. Then grasp your legs: try to hold your ankles if you can reach. Exhale, and as you do so straighten your legs; on breathing in let the knees flex again. Repeat.

SQUATS

1

2

3

▲ Stand with your feet slightly apart and raise your arms.

▲ Take your hands above your head, palms touching, and at the same time, rise up on to your toes.

▲ Slowly lower yourself into the squatting position, trying to keep your back straight. Slowly return to standing, then repeat.

STANDING TWIST

1

◀ Stand with your feet shoulder-width apart and arms raised straight out in front of you. Slowly twist your body to one side.

▶ Return to the centre, then twist from the waist to the other side. Make the movements slowly and freely.

2

BACKWARDS BEND, KNEELING

▶ Kneel on the floor, sitting on your heels. Place your hands on the floor just behind you, and raise your trunk to arch up and back as you inhale. Hold for a moment and then sink back into the kneeling position as you exhale.

MIND AND BODY: *The Balance of Tai Chi*

TAI CHI HAS BEEN VARIOUSLY DESCRIBED as a system of health, medicine, physical co-ordination, relaxation, self-defence and consciousness-raising, as well as a means of exercise and self-development. In fact, it is all these things. The style shown on the following pages is the Yang-style Short Form, as developed by Professor Cheng Man-Ch'ing, which is the most common of the various forms of Tai Chi practised in the West.

THE HISTORY OF TAI CHI

Some sources claim Tai Chi is 6000 years old, while more conservative estimates date its beginnings only a few centuries ago. It was traditionally a closely guarded secret passed down through a family. A similar art may have begun in the Tang dynasty (618–906 A.D.), but Chang San-Feng (born 1247) is generally regarded as the founder of Tai Chi, in the Sung dynasty. It is said that as a Taoist monk he saw a crane attacking a snake and was inspired by the soft and yielding nature of the snake, which eventually out-manoeuvred the crane and its hard attacking beak.

Yang Lu-Ch'an (1799–1872) was the founder of Yang style Tai Chi. Legend has it that he learned by spying on Chen Chang-Hsin teaching his students, and was soon able to beat even the advanced ones. Grandmaster Chen was so impressed that he taught Yang all the Chen family Tai Chi skills, reasoning that it was better to spread the essence of Tai Chi to the world than to risk losing its vitality by restricting it to family members only.

Yang Jien-Hou (1839–1917) was the third son of Yang Lu-Ch'an, and also became a famous exponent of Tai Chi. His third son, Yang Cheng-Fu (1883–1936), realized that Tai Chi could improve the health and lift the spirit of the entire nation: he taught Cheng Man-Ch'ing for seven years. The current Yang Forms were defined and regulated by Yang Cheng-Fu, and modified by Cheng Man-Ch'ing (1901–1975), who removed some of the repetition from the Form while retaining its essence.

Following the Cultural Revolution, many great teachers went to South-east Asia, especially Taiwan, Singapore and Malaysia. Cheng Man-Ch'ing took Tai Chi to New York in the mid-1960s and Gerda Geddes introduced it to Britain. Since then it has continued to flourish around the world.

Chinese people practise Tai Chi together in parks in the morning air.

Tai Chi for Health or Self-defence?

Although Tai Chi can eventually be used in self-defence, and most classes do incorporate some of its practical applications, it is initially practised mainly for its health-giving benefits. It is particularly useful for increasing alertness and body awareness, and for developing concentration and sensitivity. It helps with balance and posture, and enhances a sense of "groundedness". However, all the postures have a validity in defending yourself against an attack by an opponent. Its gentleness and subtlety do not preclude it being a very effective form of self-defence.

It is not easy to separate the physical and mental aspects of Tai Chi, as they are closely interrelated. In Chinese medicine, the interdependence of mind, body and spirit is seen as integral to well-being. Physical symptoms

will affect the emotions and the psyche, and mental troubles will affect your health. In Tai Chi the cat-like alertness required, the relaxed mind, the softening and opening of the joints, the balance and the flow of Chi evenly through the body are all equally important for health and self-defence.

Once you have attained these qualities, which may take many years, you can start to work on increasing the speed in order to practise applications with a partner, while still maintaining the precision, balance and relaxation that are inherent in Tai Chi.

Above: Younger children are encouraged to learn "hard" martial arts such as karate before beginning Tai Chi.
Left: Partner work often incorporates "Sticking Hands".
Facing page: "Pushing Hands".

THE THEORY OF TAI CHI

Like music, Tai Chi cannot be appreciated purely on an intellectual level. It has to be experienced in order to gain an understanding. However, it is useful to look at some of the concepts which are fundamental to the martial arts, as well as to medicine and philosophy. Although treated separately in the West, all these are inseparable in the Eastern view. From thousands of years of close observation of patterns of energy, the Chinese evolved a system of healing that can be used both as preventive medicine and for the treatment of disease.

CHI

Chi is the driving force of human life, the spark behind thought, creativity and growth which maintains and nurtures us. It can be felt as movement of energy in the body, like the flow of an electrical current.

Chi flows through the body along channels called meridians, as blood flows along arteries and veins. When there is a blockage, Chi cannot flow adequately to nourish the organs, and illness results. The concept of Chi is at the very centre of Tai Chi, which aims to restore balance so that Chi flows freely.

THE TAN TIEN

The Chi is stored in the Tan Tien. This is an area about the size of a golf ball, located four finger-widths below the navel, and about one-third of the way from the front to the back of the body. It is the centre of gravity of the body, and in Tai Chi all movement emanates from it. Try to let the breath and the mind sink to the Tan Tien.

YIN AND YANG

Yin and Yang describe the complementary yet opposing forces of nature, such as night and day, cold and hot, female and male, winter and summer, death and life.

Their relationship has a harmony and balance: both Yin and Yang are necessary, they are constantly moving and balancing each other, and the interaction between them creates Chi. The Chinese observed that when the balance of Yin and Yang is disrupted in an individual, so too will be the body's Chi, leading to ill health.

FINDING A CLASS

Tai Chi cannot be learned from a book alone (or even a video), and it's important to find a class that you feel comfortable in. You may prefer the intensity of learning with a very small group, or you may enjoy the energy created by a large one. It is important to have good sight lines in order to be able to see the teacher's movements, and sufficient space around you.

One of the joys of Tai Chi is that no special equipment or clothing is needed, simply a small area, well ventilated and with good natural light. Practise outdoors if you can, but most students are apprehensive at first and don't like to feel exposed to the elements – and curious onlookers.

Wear loose, comfortable clothing and flat-soled shoes (not trainers or sneakers), although Tai Chi can be performed in bare or stockinged feet.

The emphasis is on small amounts of regular practice, preferably a few minutes each day. Normally a new "posture" will be learned each week. Repetition and correction of the postures in class is important. Some of the adjustments made may feel only very minor, but they will be significant in allowing the Chi to circulate around the body more freely.

The scope for refining and improving your Tai Chi is limitless. Some of the great masters now in their 70s and 80s have been practising daily since they were children. Each of us needs to find our own level of practice and commitment, but one thing is certain: it cannot be hurried.

Above: Finding a good class is essential for your progress.
Below: Tai Chi slippers can be worn.

THE PRINCIPLES OF TAI CHI

When you begin you may feel awkward and clumsy. Beginners are often surprised at their lack of coordination and balance, and at the differences in mobility between their right and left sides. If you have tended to lean slightly to your left for years, when you straighten up it will feel as though you are tilted to the right. This may take a while to change. As you learn to relax and feel more comfortable with a new way of moving, the positions and steps start to feel more natural. Be patient and diligent: perfecting the moves can take a lifetime.

Tai Chi movements have been likened to a cat taking a tentative step as it walks.

body should feel light and agile, free and flexible. Your lower body should feel heavy and well grounded.

• Establish a solid "root" with the ground – imagine small roots growing from the soles of your feet into the earth.

• Align the joints of your shoulder, hip, knee and ankle vertically, so that gravity keeps your body in alignment rather than muscular effort. Never lock any of the joints.

• Let your tongue rest lightly on the roof of your mouth.

• Let your mind begin the movement, which comes up through the legs, is directed by the waist and flows out through the fingertips.

• Relax. This is the basic principle. The body needs to be loose and open so that Chi can flow freely. Allow tension to sink from your upper body down through your legs to the soles of your feet and into the earth.

• Allow your mind and your Chi to settle into the Tan Tien. Sinking your chest slightly helps this to happen. Relax your shoulders and elbows. Your upper

• Be in the present moment, focusing on what is actually happening, not thinking about the move just past or the one to come.

• Never use force. Avoid wasting energy. Let your movements be light, nimble and effortless.

• Seek stillness within movement. Seek serenity within activity.

WARM-UP EXERCISES

Perform these exercises slowly and gently, with the mind and the breath focused in the Tan Tien. Notice any differences between the right and left sides of your body, and between the upper and lower parts. Be aware of the harmonious interrelationships of all the various parts of your body as you move and breathe. Concentrate, too, on the natural expansion and contraction of your lungs, and the movement of your ribcage at the sides and back of your body as well as at the front.

All the exercises in this chapter are performed with the feet shoulder-width apart and parallel to each other unless otherwise stated. However, for those unable to stand, most of the exercises can also be done in a sitting position and great benefit can still be obtained from them.

EXERCISE 1
Circling Hands
This is a very calming exercise which may be repeated for several minutes.

1 Inhale and allow both hands to float upwards a comfortable distance in front of your body, palms facing downwards.

2 As your hands rise above your head, relax the wrists and begin to open the palms outwards.

3 As you exhale, continue to open out your arms to your sides, palms facing upwards. Draw your hands inwards at the bottom of the circle, ready to turn over and begin a new circle.

EXERCISE 2
Push to Heaven and Earth

Throughout this exercise, there is a changing relationship between the hands, whether they are facing towards or away from each other. Co-ordinate your breathing so that as the breath changes from inhalation to exhalation, or vice versa, so the hands change their direction.

1 Breathe in and let both hands float up in front of your body, palms upwards. As you exhale, your right hand pushes down towards earth, ending up by your right hip, while your left hand turns over and pushes up towards heaven, finishing above your left temple. Feel a diagonal stretch through your entire body.

2 Breathe in again, relaxing your palms which now turn to face each other and begin moving towards each other in front of your body. Feel as if there is a ball of energy between your hands.

3 Turn your right palm over and outwards as you exhale. Continue to push your right hand upwards until it arrives above your right temple, while your left hand now pushes down, finishing by your left hip.

4 Breathe in again and bring your hands in front of your body in a mirror image of Step 2.

Exercise 3
Shaking out Shoulders, Arms and Hands

▶ Gently shake out any tension in your wrists and hands. Gradually work up to include your shoulders. This exercise is especially useful before, during and after long periods at a keyboard, or for anyone who does intricate or repetitive work with the hands.

Exercise 6
Rotating Waist

▼ Place both hands lightly on your hips. Keeping your head up, begin by spiralling your hips slowly outwards, feeling for any restriction, tightness or lack of ease. Change direction and spiral back in slowly.

Exercise 4
Loosening Shoulders

◀ Make increasing circles with one shoulder. Change direction and decrease the size of the circles. Repeat for the other shoulder. Rotate your shoulders alternately.

Exercise 5
Loosening Wrists

▶ Ensure that each finger is lightly touching the thumb. The feeling should be one of holding a droplet of water. Make circles with your hands, keeping your arms and shoulders relaxed.

EXERCISE 7
Knee Rotations

1 Bring your feet together and place your palms lightly on your upper kneecaps. Feel the Chi from your palms radiating deep into your knee joints. Circle your knees clockwise several times, then change direction.

2 Keep your legs and hands in the same position. Rotate your knees in opposite directions – one circles clockwise while the other circles anti-clockwise (counter-clock-wise). Change the direction of each knee and repeat the rotations.

EXERCISE 9
Calf Stretch

◀ Turn out your left foot to 45° and step forward with your right foot. Keeping the heel on the floor, pull up your toes towards the knee. Drop your body forward, keeping your right leg straight and letting your hands hang down. Hold for a few breaths and release. Repeat for the other leg.

EXERCISE 8
Shaking Out Legs and Feet

▼ Stand on one leg while gently shaking tension from the other leg for 10–15 seconds. Repeat for the other leg.

EXERCISE 10
Four-directional Breathing

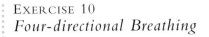

1 As you inhale, bring your hands up to chest height, palms facing upwards.

2 As you exhale, turn the palms to face away and extend your arms as if pushing something away.

3 On the next inhalation, turn your palms back to face your body, softening your arms and drawing them back in towards your chest.

4 Exhale again, turn the palms out and extend your arms out to your sides.

5 Relax and bring your arms in towards your chest as you inhale.

6 On the next exhalation turn your palms upwards and extend your arms towards the sky.

7 Breathe in again and let your arms descend, palms facing downwards.

8 As your arms and hands pass the Tan Tien, begin breathing out and pushing down towards the earth. On the next inhalation the hands come up and a new cycle of four breaths begins. Repeat this sequence several times.

EXERCISE 11
Rotating from the Waist with Feet Forward

1 Imagine a central axis from the crown of your head, dropping down through your body to a point between your feet. Rotate your body around this axis, keeping your arms relaxed. Try to keep each knee over its respective big toe, and shift your weight from one leg to the other as you turn.

2 As your waist turns to the left, your weight shifts on to your left leg. As it turns right, move your weight across on to your right leg. Let your arms swing naturally, following the movement of your waist. Repeat the sequence for about 1 minute.

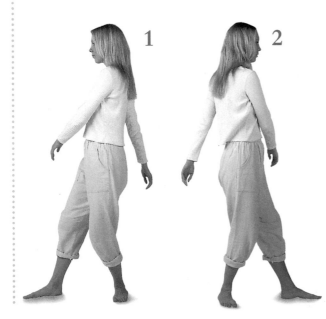

EXERCISE 12
Rotating from the Waist with Feet Pivoting on the Heel

This is similar to the previous exercise, but the weight shifts differently.

1 Bring all your weight on to your left leg and turn your waist to the right, simultaneously turning your right foot out to 90°.

2 As your waist returns to the centre, the right toes come around. The right heel remains on the ground. Then, as you turn your waist to the left, transfer your weight completely to your right leg and pivot on your left heel, turning the toes through 90°. Gradually increase the speed until you find a comfortable, gentle rhythm. Continue for about 1 minute.

EXERCISE 13
Rotating from the Waist Turning on the Ball of the Foot

In this exercise, the movement of the waist is exactly as in the previous two exercises. The arms also follow the same movement, but each foot pivots in turn on the ball.

1 Keeping your weight in your left leg, turn your waist to the right. Lift your right heel and swivel the right foot through 90°.

2 As your waist returns to the centre, straighten your right foot until your feet are parallel and shoulder-width apart. Transfer your weight on to your right foot.

3 Turn your waist to the left, lift your left heel and pivot on the ball of your left foot. Turn back to the centre and repeat the sequence for about 1 minute, keeping your head up, back straight and arms and shoulders relaxed.

EXERCISE 14
Opening and Closing the Circle

1 Place your hands in front of your face, palms facing away. Turn your waist slowly to the right.

2 Drop your weight into your right leg and continue turning your waist, which in turn brings your hands around in a large circular movement.

3 As your hands cross the bottom of the circle, shift your weight into your left leg.

4 Continue to turn your waist slowly, bringing your hands up to complete the circle.

5 When your hands reach their starting-point in front of your face, repeat the sequence and continue for several more rotations.

6 Change direction gently at the bottom of the circle to repeat the sequence. This time, join your palms together lightly at the top of each circle.

7 Keep the palms together as you turn, allowing your hands to separate at the bottom of the circle. Remember to move from the waist and transfer your weight.

8 Finish the exercise by keeping your palms connected and spiralling your hands in slowly to end in front of your chest.

Exercise 15
Arm Rotations

1 Turn out your right foot to 45° and take a shoulder-width step forwards with your left foot. Bring 70% of your weight on to your left leg, and rest your left hand on your hip. Form a loose fist with your right hand and rotate the arm backwards three times, then forwards three times in a large circle. Repeat twice.

2 Turn out your left foot to 45° and take a shoulder-width step forwards with your right foot. Bring 70% of your weight on to your right leg, and rest your right hand on your hip, in a mirror image of Step 1. Form a loose fist with your left hand and rotate the arm backwards three times, then forwards three times in a large circle. Repeat twice.

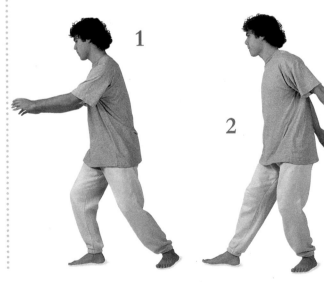

Exercise 16
Shifting Weight

1 Place your left foot at 45° and your right foot pointing forward, with heels shoulder-width apart. Shift your weight from one leg to the other, keeping the Tan Tien on a horizontal plane – do not tip your pelvis forwards or backwards.

2 Let your arms swing naturally with the momentum of the weight shifting. Continue for about 1 minute, then place your right foot at 45° with your left foot forward and repeat. Feel a strong root developing through your feet into the earth.

EXERCISE 17
Stepping Forward, Stepping Back

1 Place your left foot at 45°, right foot pointing forward. Shift all your weight from the left foot to the right, then back on to the left. With no weight on the right foot, pick it up and take a step backwards, toe first.

2 Transfer your weight to the right foot, then back to the left. Take a step forwards with the "empty" right foot, heel first. Repeat this sequence several times, concentrating on the steps being empty of any weight. Repeat the exercise, keeping the right foot rooted to the ground, and stepping with the left foot.

EXERCISE 18
Waving Hands in Clouds

1 Begin with your right hand facing the Tan Tien, your left hand directly above it, facing your chest. Slowly turn your waist to the left, shifting your weight into your left leg. At the same time turn your palms towards each other, as if holding a large ball.

2 Bring your waist back to the front. As you do so, lower your left hand until it is opposite the Tan Tien and raise your right hand to the level of your chest, with your palms facing your body.

3 Now turn your waist to the right, shift the weight across to your right leg, and turn your palms towards each other in a mirror image of Step 1. Repeat the entire sequence several times.

EXERCISE 19 *Push to Centre, Push to Corner*

1 Place your right foot at 45° and step forward with your left foot. Begin with all your weight on your right leg, right hand resting palm upwards on your right hip, left fingertips in line with your mouth, palm facing diagonally forwards and to the centre.

2 Bring your weight forward on to your left leg. Your right hand turns diagonally forwards as it comes to push towards the centre of your body; your left hand turns palm upwards as it draws back to rest on your left hip.

3 Shift your weight back on to your right foot, turning your waist 45° to the right. At the same time draw your right hand back to your right hip and push your left hand towards the corner until it is in line with the centre of your body, fingertips opposite your mouth. Repeat Steps 2 and 3 for about 1 minute.

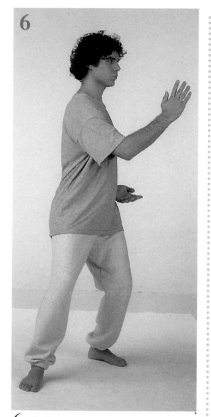

4 Repeat the sequence in mirror image. Place your left foot at 45° and step forward with the right. Begin with all your weight on your left leg, left hand resting palm upwards on your left hip, right fingertips in line with your mouth, palm facing diagonally forwards and to the centre.

5 Bring your weight forward on to your right leg. Your left hand turns diagonally forwards as it comes to push towards the centre of the body, your right hand turns palm upwards as it draws back to rest on the right hip.

6 Shift your weight back on to your left foot, turning your waist through 45° to the left. At the same time, draw your left hand back to your left hip and push your right hand towards the corner until it is in line with the centre of your body, fingertips opposite your mouth. Repeat the cycle in Steps 5 and 6 for about 1 minute.

EXERCISE 20
Rotating Whole Body, Arms in Front

1 Hold both arms horizontally in front of the chest, palms facing inwards, fingertips almost touching. You should feel as if you are holding a large ball, or "hugging a tree".

2 Turn your waist to the right, simultaneously shifting your weight across to your right leg.

3 Return to the centre, then turn to the left and move your weight on to your left leg. Move your arms with the rest of your body each time.

EXERCISE 21
Neck Rotations

▶ Keep the palms of your hands in front of and facing your chest, fingertips almost touching. Relax your shoulders and elbows. Turn your head to look first over one shoulder, then back to the centre before turning to look over the other. Repeat several times, keeping the neck movements as fluid as possible.

EXERCISE 22
Hip Rotations

▶ Turn out your left foot at 45° and sink all your weight on to it. Draw a smooth circle with your right knee, keeping the hip movement as fluid as possible. Repeat the same rotation on the other hip.

EXERCISE 23 *Ankle Rotations*

As you do this exercise, notice the difference between the right and left ankles – it's surprising to discover that there's often a considerable distinction!

▶ Place your left foot at 45°, bend your left knee and sink all your weight into your left leg. Lift your right foot and slowly rotate the ankle, describing a circle with your big toe. Repeat the exercise for the left ankle.

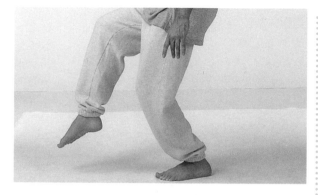

EXERCISE 24 *Return to Centre*

This exercise is the reverse of Exercise 1, "Circling Hands".

1 As you breathe in, take your hands out to the sides in front of your body, and raise them slowly in a large circle, palms facing upwards.

2 As you exhale, lower your hands in front of the centre of your body, palms facing downwards.

3 At the bottom of the circle, turn your hands outwards again to begin a new circle with the new breath.

EXERCISE 25
Stimulating the Back of the Neck

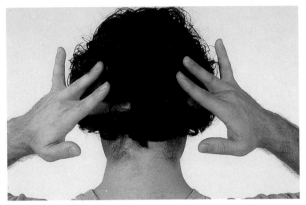

▲ Bring your heels together and turn your feet out, making a right angle at the heels. Lift your hands to the back of your head. Flick your index and middle fingers over each other to tap the base of the occipital ridge at the back of the skull, releasing Chi up to the top of your head. Flick the back of your head about 20 times.

EXERCISE 26
Kidney Massage

The kidneys are the most important organs, according to Chinese medicine, as they store the Chi, so it is important to look after them. This massage provides gentle stimulation and helps to break down crystals of uric acid, a common component of kidney stones.

▲ Bring your heels together, as in the previous exercise. Massage around your kidneys with loose fists.

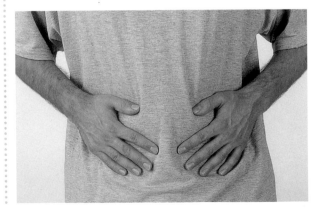

EXERCISE 27
Abdominal Massage

◀ With your heels together, massage your abdomen in a circular motion with the palms of your hands.

EXERCISE 28 *Feeling the Air*

1 With your heels together, inhale and let both hands float up towards your shoulders, palms facing upwards. Feel the resistance of the air on your palms.

2 As you exhale, let both hands float back down. Try to feel resistance on the backs of your hands, and the air rushing softly between your fingers.

EXERCISE 29
Stillness Within Movement

▶ Bring your heels together at right angles to each other. Try to feel where your body weight naturally lies. Does it tend to be greater on the left or the right foot? Is it nearer the toes or the heel? On the instep or the outer edge of the foot? Is it moving around or still? If moving, is it spiralling, circling or wandering about? Are the movements random or even, chaotic or rhythmical?

You are seeking a point of equilibrium, where you can feel relaxed, still and evenly balanced. Try to let go of any little muscular contractions and other activity. Let the weight settle gently and rest. Just let yourself be quiet and motionless. After a few quiet moments of standing still, you can begin some Tai Chi walking, or start the Form. Notice the feelings you have, especially in the Tan Tien, and carry these feelings with you into the Form.

YANG-STYLE SHORT FORM

After completing the warm-up exercises, and a moment or so quietly standing to see if you can find a point of equilibrium, a few minutes of Tai Chi walking may follow. This is walking with an "empty step", rather in the manner of a cat tentatively putting out its paw before committing its full weight to the front leg.

As you progress through the Form, use the following pages as an aide-mémoire for your practice, especially for the transitions from one posture to the next. Remember to keep your movements slow and smooth, like clouds drifting gently by on a summer's day, and - above all - relax!

Attention, Preparation and Beginning

1 Stand in a relaxed and upright posture, feet pointing diagonally outwards, making a right angle. Distribute your weight evenly.

2 Bend your right knee and sink all your weight down through your right leg into the foot, without leaning across. Move the "empty" left leg a shoulder-width away, with the toes pointing straight ahead.

3 Transfer 70% of your weight to your left leg, simultaneously turning your waist (and therefore your whole body) diagonally to the right.

4 Keeping 70% of your weight in your left leg, turn your whole body back to face the front. Bring your right foot around to the front as your waist moves. Your feet should be shoulder-width apart and parallel. Your hands also move with your body, the palms facing the ground as if resting on a cushion of air, just in front of and just below your waist.

5 Relax your wrists and let your arms float up and away from your body. When your hands reach shoulder height, gently extend the fingertips.

6 Draw your hands back in towards your body by dropping the elbows.

7 Relax your wrists and let your hands float down the front of your body, back to where they started, just in front of and just below your waist. The posture ends with another 10% of your weight sunk into your left leg, so that 80% is now in the left and 20% in the right.

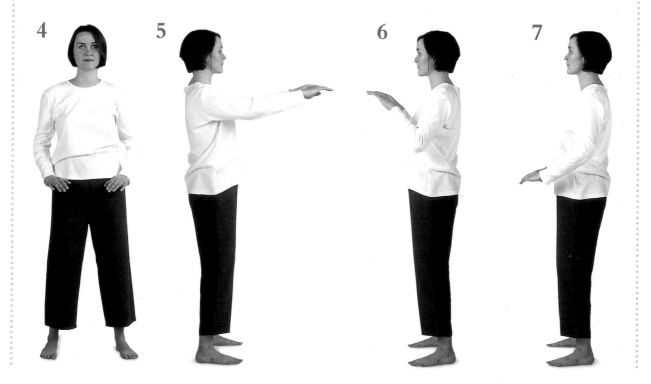

LESSON 2
Ward Off Left

1 Sink all your weight into your left leg. Turn your whole body 90° to the right, pivoting on the empty right heel. There is a feeling of holding a large ball, with the right hand in front of the chest, palm facing down, and the left hand directly under it, palm upwards.

2 Sink all your weight on to your right leg, as if carrying the ball forward. Pick up your empty left leg and step directly forward, toes pointing to the front.

3 Turn your waist to the left, to face the front. As you do so, your left hand comes up, palm facing your chest, and your right hand floats down to just outside your right thigh, palm facing down. Shift 70% of your weight into your left leg, as your right foot simultaneously comes around to 45°. If you were to draw your left foot back, your heels would be shoulder-width apart.

LESSON 3
Ward Off Right

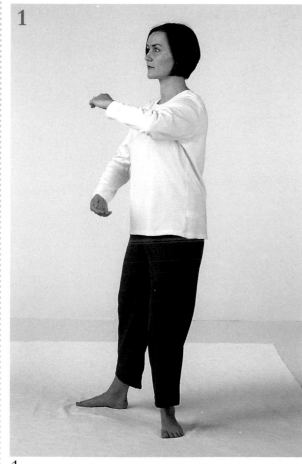

1 Sink all your weight into your left leg. Turn to the right: the left palm turns face down, the right palm turns upwards as if both hands are again holding the large ball. Pick up your right foot and step so that your heels are once more shoulder-width apart.

2 As you turn your waist to face the right-hand side, shift 70% of your weight on to your right foot, and turn your left foot to 45°. Raise your right arm so that the palm faces your chest, the fingertips of your left hand looking into the right palm.

LESSON 4
Roll Back, Press and Push
This posture, together with the one that follows it, "Single Whip", is also known as "Grasping the Sparrow's Tail".

1 Turn your body to the right. Point the fingertips of your right hand to the sky in a relaxed way. Your left arm moves horizontally with the fingertips almost touching the right elbow, palm facing the body. Your weight remains 70% on the right leg, 30% on the left.

2 As you turn your waist to the left, begin to shift weight on to your left leg. Follow the movement of the body with your arms until your right hand is horizontal. Your left hand then begins to flow down with the movement of your waist to the left. Allow all your weight to settle into your left leg.

3 Turn your waist back to the right and let your left arm follow this movement. All your weight remains in the left leg. Bring your palm across to rest against your right wrist, opposite the centre of your chest.

4 Press forward, keeping the hands in full contact. Shift 70% of your weight into your front (right) leg. Ensure that your heels are still shoulder-width apart, the right foot pointing forward, the left foot at 45°.

5 Separate your hands and sink all your weight back into your left foot. Your fingertips are now shoulder-width apart at shoulder height.

6 Move your weight forward 70% into your right leg. Your arms and hands keep the same position.

LESSON 5
Single Whip

1 As your weight shifts back into the left leg, leave your fingers where they are in space, effectively straightening – but not locking – your arms. The palms now face the ground.

2 Turn your whole body to the left and shift all your weight into your left leg. Your right heel remains on the ground while your toes turn through 120°, following the body round. Your arms remain parallel at shoulder height and shoulder-width apart.

3 Sink your weight back into your right leg. Bring your left hand under the right to hold the imaginary ball in front of your body. Meanwhile, form a "hook" with the fingers and thumb of your right hand, with the thumb connected to each finger as if holding a single droplet of water. The hook of the right hand is directly over the upturned palm of the left hand.

4 Ensure all your weight is in your right leg. Bend the right knee and turn your body to the left, sending out the hook in line with, and at the same height as, your shoulder. Take an empty shoulder-width step with your left foot, the heel connecting with the ground first. The left arm pivots at the elbow.

5 Shift 70% of your weight on to your left leg, adjusting your right foot to 45°. Ensure that your heels are shoulder-width apart, your left hand in line with your left shoulder and your right hand's hook at 90° to the rest of your body.

LESSON 6
Lifting Hands. Shoulder Stroke

1 Place all your weight on your left leg. Turn your waist to the right. Open your hands and turn the palms inwards, the left palm towards the right elbow. Pick up your empty right foot and place the heel down without weight, in such a position that if you drew the right foot back in a straight line, you would avoid clipping the left heel.

2 Turn your waist to the left, your hands following the movement of your waist. Bring your right toe by your left heel, touching the ground but weightless.

3 Take an empty shoulder-width step to the right with your right foot, heel first. Transfer 70% of your weight forwards into the right foot. Your left palm follows the weight shift to rest opposite your inner right elbow. Your right arm is curved, guarding the groin. The upper part of your right arm faces forward.

Your feet remain at right angles to each other, unlike the other postures where the rear foot has come round to 45°.

LESSON 7
White Crane Spreads Wings. Brush Left Knee and Push

1 Drop all your weight into your right leg. Turn your waist to the left. As your right hand begins to rise, your left hand sweeps down in front of your left thigh.

2 Pick up your empty left leg and touch the toe on the ground but without shifting your weight. Bring your right hand up to guard your temple, turning to face diagonally outwards as it moves up. Your left hand floats down, resting on a cushion of air outside the upper left leg.

3 As you turn your waist to the left, your right hand follows and sweeps down; your left palm opens outwards.

4 As you turn your waist to the right, your right hand continues in a circle. Your left hand follows the movement of your waist and faces palm down in front of your chest. As your waist returns to the centre, bring your right hand level with your shoulder, palm facing forwards.

5 Take a shoulder-width step with your left foot, heel first. Move 70% of your weight into your left leg as your left hand brushes down across it. Meanwhile, your right hand follows a concave curve into the centre to finish with the fingers in line with your mouth.

LESSON 8
Play Guitar. Brush Left Knee and Push
This posture is also known as "Strumming the Lute".

1 As all your weight sinks into your left leg, adjust the empty right foot by drawing it slightly nearer the left foot, toe first. Bring your weight into the right foot. Your left leg and arm float up simultaneously – imagine a thread connecting them – the left heel touching the ground but without weight. Ensure that the left leg would avoid contact with the right heel if drawn back.

2 Turn to the right, dropping your right hand down while your left hand follows the movement of your waist to the centre of your chest, palm facing down. As your waist returns to the front, your right hand comes to shoulder height, palm forwards.

3 Take a shoulder-width step with your left foot, heel first. Move 70% of your weight into your left leg as your left hand brushes down across it. Meanwhile, your right hand follows a concave curve into the centre to finish with the fingers in line with your mouth.

LESSON 9
Step Forward, Deflect Downwards, Intercept and Punch

1 Turn your waist 45° to the left and sink all your weight into your right foot. As your weight shifts back, lift the toes of your left foot and pivot 45° on the heel. Bring your hands down parallel with your left leg, just outside and in front of the thighs.

2 Shift all your weight into your left leg. Form a loose fist with your right hand as your body moves forward. Ensure that the fingers are not wrapped around the thumb. The right toes come up behind the left heel.

3 Arc both hands and your right foot simultaneously towards the centre line, as your waist turns to the right. The right foot lands empty, in line with the left instep.

4 Continue to turn your waist to the right, bringing the right fist palm upwards to rest on the right hip. Transfer all your weight to your right foot.

5 Place your left foot a shoulder width from the right foot. Shift 70% of your weight to your left leg and bring your right fist forward to punch, rotating it through a quarter turn in a corkscrew motion. Bring your left arm across your body, palm facing your inner right elbow.

LESSON 10
Withdraw and Push.
Crossing Hands

1 As you turn your waist to the left, your right arm follows your body to an angle of 45° and the fist opens up. Meanwhile, cup your left hand under your right elbow.

2 Draw your right arm across your left palm as your weight sinks into your right foot and your waist turns to the right.

3 Bring your waist back to the centre and turn both palms to face the front.

4 Move your weight forward 70% on to your left leg. Your hands remain at shoulder width and shoulder height.

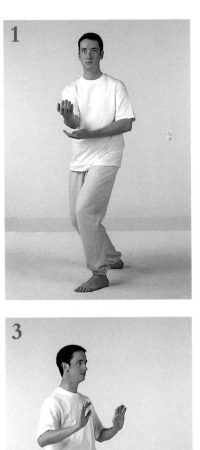

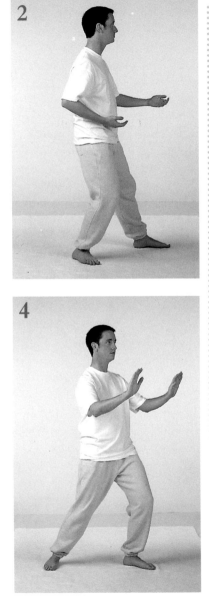

5 Turn your waist to the right and simultaneously sink all your weight into your left leg. Draw your hands in towards your chest in a softly inverted "V" shape, as if holding the top of a large ball.

6 As your whole weight shifts into your right leg, turn your waist to the right. Your left toes turn with your waist and your right hand travels out diagonally upwards.

7 Sink all your weight back into your left leg. Your left hand now travels out diagonally.

8 Bring your right foot shoulder–width away from and parallel to the left, but maintain your weight 70% in the left leg. Both hands circle down and up, stopping opposite your chest, palms facing the body. The wrists are touching, with the right wrist outside the left one.

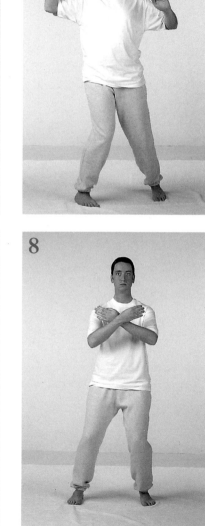

LESSON 11
Embrace Tiger, Return to Mountain

1 Keeping all your weight in your left leg, turn your waist to the right, pivoting on the ball of your right foot. Open your hands outwards. Step diagonally back with your right foot. Ensure the step is empty, and that the heels are shoulder-width apart. Move your weight 70% on to your right foot. As your waist completes its turn to the right diagonal, move your left hand so that the fingertips are in line with your left shoulder, palm facing forward. The right hand is palm up by the hip.

2 As you turn your waist slightly to the right, allow your left hand to come across so that the fingertips point to your right elbow. Meanwhile, your right hand travels upwards so that the fingertips point heavenward.

LESSON 12
Roll Back, Press and Push: Diagonal Single Whip

▼ Now repeat the sequence "Grasping the Sparrow's Tail" in Lessons 4 and 5. This time, perform this section from one diagonal corner to the other rather than from one side to the other. This picture shows your position at the end of the sequence, facing the corner.

LESSON 13
Punch under Elbow

1 Sink all your weight back on to your right foot. Turn your waist 45° to the left, lifting the left toes and letting your left foot and both arms pivot 45° to the left.

2 Lower your left foot, gradually shifting weight forward into it. When all your weight is on your left foot, step forward with your right foot so that the heel is in line with your left instep.

3 Rotate your upper body 90° to the left. Your arms follow this waist movement, so that the hook (your right hand) is now out in front level with your right shoulder, and your left hand is level with your face at 90° to the front. Your weight is in your left leg.

4 Transfer all your weight to your right leg, turning your waist to the right and letting your left hand move down, then up, until the fingers are in line with your left shoulder. Your left arm and leg move around simultaneously. Rest your left heel on the ground without any weight. Meanwhile, turn your right hand into a loose fist and draw it towards your body to rest just inside your left elbow.

LESSON 14
Step Back to Repulse the Monkey: Right and Left

1 As you turn your waist further to the right, your right hand opens and moves down by your hip, then floats up to shoulder height. The palm of your left hand turns over to face down. Your eyes remain midway between your palms, with both hands staying in your peripheral vision.

2 Step back with your left foot as your waist turns to the left. Your right hand travels forward, palm facing down, while your left hand travels down towards your left hip with the palm facing upwards.

3 Feel the connection between the palms as your hands pass near each other. The right toes also straighten as the waist turns. As you continue to turn to the left, your left hand floats up to shoulder height, while your right hand comes forward, palm facing down, in a mirror image of Step 1.

LESSON 15
Step Back to Repulse the Monkey (Right).
Diagonal Flying

1 Turn your waist to the right, step back with your right foot and let your left hand travel forward, palm down. Your right hand moves down to rest on your hip, palm up. Your left foot turns to face the front as the waist moves. Your right hand now comes up to shoulder height, palm down, to return to the posture shown in Step 1 of Lesson 14 opposite.

2 With your weight on your left foot, turn your waist to the left. Turn your right hand palm upwards as it travels round in front of your waist, while your left hand, palm downwards, comes in front of your chest. Your hands are now holding an imaginary ball in front of your chest, with the left hand uppermost and the right hand directly below it.

3 Turn your waist 90° to the right, maintaining the position of your arms and hands in front of your chest, as if carrying the ball.

4 Stepping with your right foot, turn a further 135° to the right, and transfer 70% of your weight into the right foot. Your waist also turns to the right and your right hand moves with it, travelling to shoulder height, arm extended and facing diagonally upwards. Your left hand moves simultaneously to just outside your left thigh, palm facing down.

LESSON 16
Waving Hands in Clouds (Right, Left, Right)

1 Bring all your weight on to your right foot. Turn your waist to the right and move your left hand across near your right hip. At the same time, your right hand turns palm downwards at shoulder height. Raise your left foot and move it forward until the left heel is level with the right.

2 As your waist turns to the front, move your right hand to face it and your left hand to face your chest. The right toes swivel round to face forwards so that your feet are now shoulder-width apart.

3 As your waist turns to the left, turn your palms towards each other, as if holding a large ball to the left of your body. All your weight is in your left leg and your right foot steps in to half shoulder width.

4 Turn your waist back to the centre. Your hands again change position, the left hand descending to be opposite and facing your waist, and the right hand opposite and facing your chest.

5 Turn your waist to the right, your hands holding the imaginary ball, with the right hand uppermost, palm facing down, and the left hand below it, palm facing up. When all your weight is on your right foot, step back to shoulder width with the left.

LESSON 17
Waving Hands in Clouds (Left, Right, Left). Single Whip

1 Turn your waist back to the centre, bringing your right hand down to face your waist and your left hand up to face your chest. Repeat Steps 3, 4 and 5, then Steps 2 and 3 from Lesson 16.

2 Turn your waist back to the centre and form a hook with your right hand, as it moves in level with your chest, directly above your left hand which is located in front of your waist, palm upwards.

3 Step forward with your right foot. Turn your waist to the right, then to the left as you transfer your weight to your right foot, sending out the hook at 90° to the front of your body.

4 Continue turning your waist to the left and step with your left foot to shoulder width, with your left palm facing your left shoulder.

5 Shift your weight 70% on to your left foot, turning away your left palm at shoulder height, and turning the right toes to 45°.

LESSON 18
Golden Rooster Stands on One Leg (Left). Squatting Single Whip

1 Sink all your weight into your left leg, turning your left hand over so that the palm faces upwards. Simultaneously turn out the right toes.

2 Move your weight across into your right leg, bringing your left palm in towards your chest. The left toes turn 45° to the right.

3 Sink down into your right leg, keeping your back straight. Move your waist to the left, brush open your left knee with your left arm and turn your left toes out 90° to the left.

4 Transfer all your weight into your left leg. Open the right hand hook, lower the hand then bring it up in front of your chest. Raise your right leg as your weight shifts forward into your left leg, so that your right thigh becomes parallel with the ground. Bend your left knee and let your left hand rest on a cushion of air by your left thigh.

LESSON 19
Golden Rooster Stands on One Leg (Right). Separate Right Foot

1 Place your right foot down and move all your weight on to it. As your weight sinks into your right leg, your right hand descends to rest on a cushion of air by your right thigh. Your left arm and left leg simultaneously move up to form a mirror image of the previous posture.

2 Step out with your empty left foot diagonally to the left, and form a ward-off position with your left arm horizontally across your body opposite your chest.

3 Shift all your weight into your left leg, bringing your right arm up to cross in front of your left arm, with the wrists touching. Bring your right toe to your left heel. Turn your wrists, maintaining skin contact as you do so, so that your left arm now crosses your right.

4 Then turn your hands away from your body, and open them out in a fan-like action.

5 Keep your left hand level with your left ear, palm facing away. Open out your right hand to the corner, below shoulder height, and simultaneously kick gently with your right leg, to knee height.

Lesson 20
Separate Left Foot. Brush Left Knee and Push

1 Keeping all your weight in your left leg, turn to the left-hand corner, forming a ward-off position with your right arm.

2 Turn your waist to the right and step to the right with your right leg. As you transfer weight into it, bring your left hand up outside the right so that the wrists meet. The left toes come to the right heel.

3 Open out your hands, the right hand this time remaining level with the head and the left hand travelling to below shoulder height. The left foot follows, kicking gently to the corner.

4 Turn your waist and left knee to the front again. Take a shoulder-width empty step with your left leg, toes pointing forwards.

5 Brush your left hand across and above the front of your left leg, to just outside your left thigh. Your right hand curves in, fingertips forward, to finish with the fingers in line with your mouth.

LESSON 21
Needles at Sea Bottom

1 Move all your weight into your left leg. Pick up your empty right foot and make a small adjustment step forward.

2 Place your right toes down, then as you sink your weight into the foot, bring your left hand across your body so that the left palm rests above your right wrist. At the same time, pick up your left leg and place the toes down empty of any weight: all your weight is now in your right leg.

3 Move your right arm forwards and diagonally downwards with your body, then vertically downwards. The arm remains in line with your right leg, and all your weight remains in your right leg.

LESSON 22
Iron Fan Penetrates Back. Turn Body, Chop and Push

1 As you raise your body, your weight remains in your right leg and both hands assume a ward-off position. Take a shoulder-width step with the left foot. Shift your weight 70% into your left leg and turn your hands outwards, the left hand in front of your mouth, the right hand guarding your temple.

2 Turn your waist to the right and sink all your weight back into your right leg, bringing your left toes round. Bring your left hand up, turning the palm diagonally outwards to guard the temple. At the same time, form a loose fist with your right hand, palm facing downwards in front of your chest.

3 Sink all your weight back on to your left leg. As you transfer the weight back, the fist descends in front of your groin.

4 Step to shoulder width with your right foot. Your right arm pivots at the elbow and your left arm folds across so that the left hand faces the right inner elbow. All your weight remains on your left leg.

5 Transfer your weight forward 70% into your right leg. Your left arm pushes forward, fingertips in line with your left shoulder, and your right fist descends to your right hip, palm upwards. The left toes are at 45°.

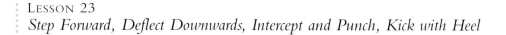

LESSON 23
Step Forward, Deflect Downwards, Intercept and Punch, Kick with Heel

1 Sink all your weight back into your left leg as your waist turns to the left. Bring the right toe to the left heel. Your right hand comes across your body, the fist softens and the palm faces down by the left hip. The left hand is directly below the right hand, palm upwards. Now go back to Lesson 9 and repeat Steps 3, 4 and 5.

2 Sink your weight into your left leg, turning your waist to the right. Cross your wrists, the right outside the left. Sink your weight back into your right leg. Your waist turns left and your left foot pivots on the heel 45° to the left. Shift all your weight forward into your left leg, turning your hands palms outwards.

3 Open your hands out like a fan, the right hand to below shoulder height, the left hand at head height, palms facing away. Your right foot comes up from the ground and the heel kicks diagonally away.

LESSON 24
Brush Right Knee and Push. Brush Left Knee and Punch Down

1 Place your empty right foot on the ground, toes forward. Your right hand curves down to rest on a cushion of air outside your right thigh. Your left hand curves forward to push to the centre, fingertips in line with your mouth.

2 Sink back into your left leg, turning your waist to the right, the palm of your left hand facing your body in a ward-off position.

3 Transfer your weight forward into your right foot, with your left palm turning downwards.

4 When all your weight is in your right foot, take an empty shoulder-width step with your left foot, and bring 70% of your weight into it. Your right hand forms a loose fist, which comes up over your right hip and punches down into the centre. Your left hand brushes across your left leg and rests outside your left knee. Your back remains straight.

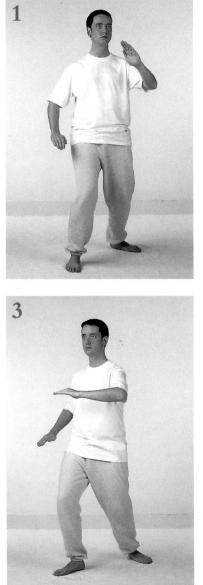

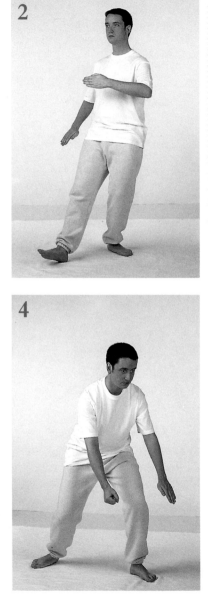

LESSON 25
*Ward Off Right. Roll Back,
Press and Push. Single Whip*

1 Sink back into your right leg. Your left hand assumes a ward-off position, the fingertips of your right hand pointing towards the centre of the left palm. Your right palm faces downwards.

2 Turn your body 45° to the left, pivoting on the left heel. Shift all your weight forward into your left leg. Your left arm remains in position, while your right hand presses down.

3 Step through at shoulder width with your empty right foot. As you transfer 70% of your weight into it, your right hand comes up into a ward-off position opposite your chest, with the left fingertips now pointing towards the right palm, left palm downwards. Now repeat Lessons 4 and 5.

LESSON 26
Fair Lady Weaves Shuttles (Right and Left)

1 Transfer your weight to your right leg as you turn your waist to the right, and turn the empty left toes through 90°. Bring your left hand across your body and under your elbow. Open the hook of your right hand and lower the right arm, palm turning upwards.

2 Sink your weight back into your left leg, turn your waist further to the right and turn out your right foot so the heel is in line with the left instep.

3 Sink your weight into your right leg, drawing your left arm across your right palm, and step at shoulder width to the left corner with your left foot. As you shift your weight forward into your left leg, turn both palms outwards, the left hand guarding your temple and the right in line with your mouth.

4 Transfer your weight into your right foot and turn your waist and left foot to the right as far as possible (135°). Turn your palms to face your body, the right palm by the left elbow.

5 Sink your weight back into your left leg and draw your left arm across your right palm.

6 Turn a further 135° right, to the corner. Step to shoulder width with your right foot, and shift 70% of your weight into it, pushing towards the centre of your mouth with your left hand. Bring your right hand up to guard your forehead, palm facing diagonally outwards.

LESSON 27
Fair Lady Weaves Shuttles (Right and Left)

1 Turn your waist 45° to the left, sinking all your weight into your left leg. Pick up your empty right foot and draw it inwards, toes pointing to the front. Transfer all your weight to your right foot, then step to the left corner (45°) with your left foot. Turn your palms in again and draw your right arm across the left palm, left arm remaining in a ward-off position.

2 Your left hand then moves up and turns outwards by your head, while the fingers of your right hand come into the centre in line with your mouth. Now repeat the postures described in Steps 4, 5 and 6 of Lesson 26.

Ward Off Left. Ward Off Right. Roll Back,
Press and Push. Single Whip

1 Sink your weight into your left leg as your waist turns to the left. Both arms come round with the movement of your waist, the left hand marginally lower than the right. The right toes come round to 45° from the front.

2 Sink your weight into your right leg as your left hand presses down, palm facing downwards. Take a shoulder-width step with your left foot.

3 Transfer your weight 70% into your left foot. Your left hand comes up in front of your chest, palm facing the body in a ward-off position. Your right hand floats on a cushion of air outside your right thigh. Now repeat the postures described in Lessons 3, 4 and 5.

LESSON 29
Squatting Single Whip, Step Forward to the Seven Stars

1 Repeat the postures described in Steps 1, 2 and 3 of Lesson 18, ending by brushing open the left knee.

2 Transfer all your weight into your left leg. The right hand hook opens and the hand descends, then comes up in front of your neck, where it forms a loose fist. At the same time, your left hand rises up to form a loose fist, and connects at the wrist inside your right hand. Move your right toes forward to touch the ground without weight.

LESSON 30
Step Back to Ride Tiger.
Turn Body and Sweep Lotus
with Leg

1 Keep your weight in your left leg and step back with your right foot, toes touching the ground first. Sink your weight into it and turn your waist to the right. The fists open and then move down by your right hip, wrists still connected.

2 Pick up your left leg as your waist turns right, then place your toes down as your waist turns back to the left. Your right hand comes around to the front with the movement of your waist, fingertips level with your right ear, and your left hand sweeps down across your body and left leg, to rest outside your left thigh.

3 Pick up your left toes, turn your waist to the left corner and place the toes down empty of any weight. Your right palm faces your inner left elbow. Your left hand is at the height of your left shoulder, elbow relaxed.

4 Lift your left toes and swing your waist clockwise, pivoting on the ball of your right foot. Your arms swing round to the right with the movement of your waist.

5 Drop your left foot and transfer all your weight into it straight away.

6 When your arms and waist reach the front (the arms at shoulder height and shoulder width with the palms facing downwards), your right foot lifts up and circles clockwise.

7 After circling, your right leg comes to rest with the upper leg parallel to the ground and foot relaxed. Your left leg is bent.

LESSON 31
*Bend Bow to Shoot Tiger.
Step Forward, Deflect
Downwards, Intercept and
Punch*

1 Turn your waist to the right.
Your arms follow your waist,
dropping down parallel, and your
right foot is placed facing the right
corner.

2 As your waist turns to the right,
shift your weight into your right
leg and circle your arms round to
the right of your waist. As your
waist turns back to the left, raise
your arms and circle round with
the waist movement. Form loose
fists with both hands. Bring the
right hand up to the right of your
forehead, knuckles facing your
right eyebrow. Your left hand
remains at shoulder height.
Continue turning your waist to
the left, keeping all your weight in
your right leg. Pick up your
empty left foot and make a small
adjustment step, the toe returning
to the ground first.

3 Sink your weight into your left
leg and pick up your right foot,
placing the toes by your left heel.
Open the left fist as your arms
move across your body following
the waist movement.

4 Both hands and your right foot
simultaneously arc towards the
centre line, as your waist turns to
the right. The right foot lands
empty, in line with the left instep.

5 Continue to turn your waist,
bringing the right fist palm
upwards to rest on your right hip
and shifting all your weight on to
your right foot. Step through at
shoulder width with your left foot.
Now shift 70% of your weight to
the left leg and bring your right
fist forward to punch, rotating
through a quarter turn in a
corkscrew motion. Your left arm
comes across your body, palm
facing your inner right elbow.

LESSON 32
Withdraw and Push. Crossing Hands. Conclusion, Attention

1 Repeat the postures described in Lesson 10. Ensure your weight is 70% in your left leg when crossing hands.

2 From crossing hands, turn both palms down to face the ground as your body rises up.

3 Bring all your weight into your left leg, turn your waist to the right and pivot on your left heel, turning the foot out to 45°.

4 Move all your weight into your right leg. Step in with your left foot so that the feet make a right angle with each other. Bring 50% of your weight back to the left foot. Rest your arms and hands naturally by the side of your body, with your shoulders relaxed. You are now ready to begin again!

Useful Addresses

MEDITATION

UK

Gateway Books
The Hollies
Wellow
Bath
Somerset
BA2 8QJ

Western Zen Retreats
Winterhead Hill Farm
Shipham
Winscombe
Somerset
BS25 1RS

Transcendental Meditation
Freepost
London
SW1P 4YY

The Community Health Foundation
188 Old Street
London
EC1V 9FR

USA

Institute of Noetic Sciences
PO Box 909
Sausalito
CA 94966

First Zen Institute of America
113E 30th Street
New York
NY 10016

American Buddhist Association
1151 West Leland Avenue
Chicago
IL 60640

Greater Washington DC Association
of Professionals Practising the
Transcendental Meditation Program
4818 Montgomery Lane
Bethesda
MD 20814

AUSTRALASIA

Transcendental Meditation Centre
68 Wood Street
Manly
Sydney
NSW 2095

The Barry Long Centre
Box 5277
Gold Coast MC
Queensland 4217

Transcendental Meditation Centre
New Zealand
5 Adam Street
Green Lane
Auckland 5

YOGA

UK

Iyengar Yoga Institute
223a Randolph Avenue
London
W̃9 1NL

Manchester & District Institute of
Iyengar Yoga
134 King Street
Dukinfield
Tameside
Greater Manchester
M60 8HG

Edinburgh Iyengar Yoga Centre
195 Bruntsfield Place
Edinburgh
EH10 4DQ

The British Wheel of Yoga
1 Hamilton Place
Boston Road
Sleaford
Lincolnshire
NG24 7EI

USA
Satchidananda Ashram – Yogaville
Buckingham
VA 23921

International Yoga Association
92 Main Street
Warrenton
VA 20186

BKS Iyengar Yoga National
Association of the United States Inc.
8223 West Third Street
Los Angeles
CA 90038

Sivanda Yoga Vedanta Center
1246 Bryn Mawr
Chicago
IL 60660

AUSTRALASIA
BKS Iyengar Association of Australasia
1 Rickman Avenue
Mosman
NSW 2088

Sivananda Yoga Vedanta Centre
409th Avenue
Katoomba
NSW 2780

TAI CHI

UK
Tai Chi Union of Great Britain
69 Kilpatrick Gardens
Clarkston
Glasgow
Scotland
G76 7RF

Golden Rooster Tai Chi School
19 Albany Road
London
N4 4RR

Rainbow Tai Chi Kung Centre
Creek Farm
Pitley Hill
Woodland Ashburton
Devon
PQ13 7JY

British Tai Chi Chuan & Kung Fu
Association
28 Linden Farm Drive
Countesthorpe
Leicestershire
LE8 5SX

USA
Mind, Body, Spirit Academy
PO Box 415
Chadsford
PA 19317

Tai Chi Cultural Centre
PO Box 8885
Stanford
CA 94309

Sarasota Shaolia Academy
4655 Flatbush Avenue
Sarasota
Florida
FL 34233-1920

AUSTRALASIA
Australian Academy of Tai Chi
686 Parrametta Road
Croydon
NSW 2132

Shaolin Wahnan Tai Chi
RSD Strathfelsaye Road
Victoria 3551

INDEX

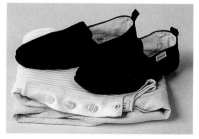